REASONABLE
ATHEISM

REASONABLE
ATHEISM

A Moral Case for
Respectful Disbelief

Scott F. Aikin & Robert B. Talisse

Prometheus Books

59 John Glenn Drive
Amherst, New York 14228–2119

Published 2011 by Prometheus Books

Inquiries should be addressed to
Prometheus Books
59 John Glenn Drive
Amherst, New York 14228–2119
VOICE: 716–691–0133
FAX: 716–691–0137
WWW.PROMETHEUSBOOKS.COM

15 14 13 12 11   5 4 3 2 1

Library of Congress Cataloging-in-Publication Data

Aikin, Scott F.
    Reasonable atheism : a moral case for respectful disbelief / by Scott F. Aikin and Robert
B. Talisse.
        p. cm.
    Includes bibliographical references and index.
    ISBN 978–1–61614–383–1 (pbk.)
    1. Atheism. 2. Ethics. I. Talisse, Robert B. II. I. Title.

BL2747.3.A34 2011
211'.8—dc22

                                                                    2010049344

For our parents:

Jean Aikin
Royace Aikin

Pat Talisse
Bob Talisse

He who knows only his own side of the case knows little of that.
—John Stuart Mill

CONTENTS

✣

Preface   9

1. Arguing in Mixed Company   15

2. What Atheism Is   43

3. On the New Atheism   67

4. Ethics without God   95

5. A Moral Case for Atheism   127

6. Religion in Politics   165

Appendix A: The Problem of Hell   193

Appendix B: The Religion and Morality Test   201

Works Cited and Further Reading   209

Index   213

PREFACE

This is a book about atheism written by two atheist philosophers. It has been written primarily for religious believers. Its aim is not to demonstrate that religious belief is silly or that religious believers are deluded. Rather, we aspire to show religious believers that atheism is a morally and intellectually responsible position. To be more precise, our aspiration is to show that the same moral commitments that religious believers place at the core of their religious conviction can be appealed to in making a case for atheism. If we succeed, we will have made a case to religious believers for thinking that atheists can be honest, sincere, intelligent, and morally responsible fellow citizens. Given the current state of democratic politics in the United States and elsewhere, this would constitute a major advance.

As we began to write the book, we naturally met with various presses and editors to discuss the prospects for publication. With one exception, the response to the idea of atheists writing for religious believers was unconditionally negative. We were told flatly that this book would have no audience. They said that religious believers want to learn about atheism from other religious believers and will not read a book by atheists. They also said that atheists read anti-religion books and will not read a book about atheism that does not aim to expose the delusions of religion and the foolishness of religious believers. Perhaps they are right and the fact that you are right now reading this book is some kind of fluke. We hope not. That is, we hope that our intellectual culture has not yet become so debased that it has become impossible to see how one could be wrong about very important matters yet not be stupid, ignorant, or foolish. We hope it is still possible for religious believers and atheists to see each other as positively wrong yet nevertheless sincere, well-intentioned, intelligent, and deserving of respect. To be sure, we, the authors, are atheists. And if you, the reader, are a religious believer, we think your religious beliefs are false. But having false beliefs doesn't make you stupid or deluded. It just makes you wrong. If you are a religious believer, you surely hold that atheists are wrong. That's fine. Our task in this book is not to settle the debate between atheists and religious believers but rather to propose a way in which fruitful debate can commence.

As we have said, this book does not aim to prove to religious believers that their religious beliefs are false. The aim instead is to show that religious believers' beliefs about *atheists* are false. Put otherwise, we aim to show that religious believers who believe that atheists must be dishonest, irrational, amoral, untrustworthy, mean, deceitful, delusional, and unintelligent have false beliefs about atheists. To be sure, individual atheists— like individual religious believers—may embody any or all of these unfortunate traits. Our argument is not that being an atheist makes one a splendid person, but that being an atheist does not make one a bad person. The difference between bad and good people does not turn on their religious beliefs or lack thereof. The goodness and badness of people is a matter of their conduct and character, not their views about religion.

Nonetheless, we realize that we have a tough row to hoe. In the United States, religious believers tend to believe the worst about atheists. We are generally believed to be immoral, dishonest, irresponsible, untrustworthy, and worst of all unfit for parenthood, citizenship, and public office. Our attempt to reverse these sentiments will proceed across the following six chapters in roughly three steps.

The first order of business is to make a case for the very project of engaging with those with whom one disagrees over important matters. There is a strong incentive to talk about the most important things only with those whom we know are inclined to agree with what we say. In chapter 1, we will argue that this is a bad policy. Importantly, our argument does not turn on some claim concerning the importance of diversity, the value of respecting the full range of belief systems, or any similar nonsense. Our case for engaging with those with whom one disagrees is a decidedly *cognitive* case. We must engage with others if we are to show due concern for the truth of our beliefs. Disengagement, we believe, is cognitively irresponsible.

Our second task is to present a version of atheism that derives from the standard moral principles typically enlisted as the basis for religious belief. Our second chapter spells out the version of atheism that we endorse and engages in additional stage-setting concerning our cognitive responsibilities as rational creatures. In our third chapter, we appeal to our position concerning our cognitive responsibilities in raising a few criticisms of the New Atheists. Our fourth and fifth chapters present the main argument of this book. It is typically thought that only those who believe in God can be moral, because all morality presupposes or requires God. In chapter 4, we argue that the thesis that God is the necessary foundation for morality is confused. God's existence is entirely irrelevant to morality. We then argue that many of the most promising accounts of morality do not require religious belief, and thus that atheists can accommodate all the usual thoughts about objective good and evil, and right and wrong. In chapter 5, we complete our main argument by showing that atheists have compelling *moral* reasons to deny God's existence and reject religious belief. Our primary claim is that one must be an atheist to take objective good and evil seriously.

The third and final step in the book is to address issues pertaining to religion in politics. In our sixth chapter, we address this issue. We argue that a proper understanding of the moral requirements for legitimate government and responsible citizenship entails a conception of democracy that affords a very limited role to religion. Indeed, we present a case for thinking that a social order that recognizes only a limited role for religion in politics is one that can show a proper regard for religious belief.

In addition to the main text, we have included two appendices. In each, we try to present the religious believer with a puzzle that arises naturally out of common religious convictions. The point of these appendices is not to advance our case with respect to atheism but to show to the religious believer that there are difficult philosophical questions one can ask from within one's own system of religious beliefs. Our view is that any sincere religious believer must grapple with such questions, even when holding firm to one's convictions.

If we had to put the main thesis of the book in a nutshell, it would go as follows. Religious believers must regard atheists in roughly the same way that they regard those who subscribe to religious faiths different from their own. There is no reason, in other words, for religious believers to regard atheists as morally suspect or dangerous. For, if our arguments are correct, there is likely to be no greater moral distance between any given religious believer and an average atheist than there is between any two average religious believers of different faiths. Accordingly, the common attitudes that religious believers have toward atheists are unwarranted and need to be abandoned.

Although this book is authored by two academics and deals with subjects that are the mainstay of professional philosophy, we have tried to write in a way that is accessible and engaging to a nonacademic audience. As part of this effort, we have abandoned the usual practice of providing extensive scholarly documentation in the form of footnotes and other apparatus. We quote original sources when necessary, but we have avoided engaging in the kind of scholarly activity that typically fills pages of notes at the end of academic books. We have elected to instead provide at the book's end a list of some of the more compelling philosophical works dealing with the issues raised in these pages. Every work mentioned or discussed in this book is listed there, along with other works that are especially germane to the topics addressed herein. Anyone wishing to continue thinking about these matters should consult our list.

In writing this book, we benefitted from the support of many friends and colleagues. We would like to thank Jeff Adams, Jason Aleksander, Theano Apostolou, Jody Azzouni, Bryan Baird, James Bednar, Antonio Bendezu, Joanne Billett, Whitney Booth, Steven Cahn, Michael Calamari, Caleb Clanton, Allen Coates, Matthew Cotter, Joan Forry, Susan Foxman, Lenn Goodman, Dwight Goodyear, David Miguel Gray, Michael Harbour, Michael Hodges, Julie Hwang, Betsy Jelinek, Mason Marshall, David McCullough, Jonathan Neufeld, Yvonne Raley, Brian Ribeiro, John Ronnholm, Aaron Simmons, Peter Simpson, Donna Smera, Robert Tempio, and Jeffrey Tlumak for helpful discussion during the composition of the manuscript. We also thank Nicole Heller and Dee Stiffler for their editorial assistance in preparing the final version of the text. This book was written with the support of a generous Research Scholar Grant from Vanderbilt University. Parts of chapter 5 borrow from Scott Aikin's "The Problem of Worship," published in *Think* (vol. 23, 2010). Appendix B, "The Religion and Morality Test," derives from Scott Aikin and Brian Ribeiro's "A Consistency Challenge for Moral and Religious Beliefs," published in *Teaching Philosophy* (vol. 32, 2009).

CHAPTER ONE

ARGUING IN MIXED COMPANY

I. GIVING MOM HER DUE

I t is impolite to discuss matters of religion or politics in mixed company. So goes the popular adage that we were supposed to have learned as children from our mothers. Let's call it *Mom's Maxim*. In this book, we will deliberately violate Mom's Maxim. We will discuss both religion *and* politics. Indeed, in our final chapter, we will go further to discuss the place of religion *in* politics. To make matters worse, we write with the hope of attracting readers who are disposed to disagree with us. That is, in writing this book, we are explicitly seeking out mixed company with whom to have a discussion about religion, politics, and their combination. We're out to start an argument. What will our mothers think?

Let's give Mom her due. As with most pearls of folk wisdom, there is some truth to Mom's Maxim. The adage enjoins us to avoid being impolite, especially in our dealings with strangers. And that certainly is sound advice. Impoliteness consists of acting in ways that make others needlessly uncomfortable or ill at ease. Although it is almost never a serious moral wrong, impoliteness is typically easy to avoid, and thus it ordinarily ought to be avoided. We are to steer clear of discussions of religion and politics, it seems, because such discussion makes others uncomfortable. To be more precise, Mom's Maxim instructs us to avoid discussion of such topics in *mixed company*, that is, among those who, for all we know, may not agree with what we say. Presumably the idea is that people are likely to hold differing political and religious views, and disagreement over these topics makes people uncomfortable. Since we generally should avoid needlessly making others uncomfortable, those topics should be taken off the table. It's that simple.

Notice, however, that there is no prohibition against argument in general. There is no adage directing us to shun discussion of other controversial matters in mixed company. People tend to hold differing views about sports, food, movies, music, novels, fashion, art, and a whole lot else. Disagreements over these topics are often heated. Yet there is no corresponding rule against discussions of *these* topics. Why is that?

Here's a possible explanation. Not all disagreement is created equal. Disagreement over certain kinds of topics, even if heated, is tolerable, whereas disagreement about other matters is less so. For example, Alfred might disagree with Betty over the artistic merits of a particular painting or the athletic talents of a particular quarterback. Their conversations about these topics may grow intense, perhaps impassioned. But, when all is said and done, they can simply put aside their differences and get on with their lives. We have a colleague who believes that Woody Allen is a greater filmmaker than Martin Scorsese, and that's OK by us. We believe she's wrong. But we can live with her error. She believes that we're wrong in our judgment that Scorsese is the better filmmaker, but she's willing to take note of our mistake and move on. On certain occasions, we argue with her; we provide our reasons for thinking that Scorsese is the better director, and she responds with criticisms of our reasons and reasons for her own view of the matter. So far, neither party has been able to convince the other. But it's OK. She's still our colleague, and we're all quite friendly.

Perhaps you think that arguments over the merits of paintings, quarterbacks, and filmmakers are silly because these are merely matters of opinion, topics about which there is no right and wrong (or true and false) view. You may think that no one person's view about these issues is better than anyone else's and that each is entitled to his or her own opinion. If with respect to paintings, quarterbacks, and filmmakers no one's view is better than anyone else's, then disagreement and argument over these matters is a waste of time. Disagreement makes sense only when there is a right answer concerning the matter in dispute or when some answers are better than others. This seems to be a popular view.

Although we, the authors, certainly agree that each is entitled to his or her own opinion, we also contend that with respect to paintings, quarterbacks, and filmmakers, some views are better—better supported, more defensible, closer to the truth—than others. We think that there are truths about these matters. We believe, for example, that Scorsese is *in fact* a better filmmaker than Allen, and that the belief that Scorsese is better than Allen is *objectively* true. Hence we think it is not a waste of time to argue with others about these topics. But we need not be detained by the philosophical quandary concerning which topics admit of objective truth. If you hold the view that beliefs about the merits of paintings, quarterbacks, and filmmakers are neither true nor false, then simply think of a case about which you do hold that some beliefs are better than others. Think of questions about which you'd say that disagreement isn't silly. Now think of disagreements of that kind that fit the description of the disagreements mentioned above; you take yourself to be right and your opponent to be mistaken, but you're not losing sleep over his or her error.

Our point is that some disagreements are such that we can live with them. You hold your view, you hold that those who disagree with you are mistaken, and you may even engage in lively debate with your opponents when the opportunity arises. But if your arguments fail to persuade, you lose no sleep over the fact that your opponents are mistaken. You can live with the fact that they're wrong, just as they can live with what they perceive as your error. Life goes on. No sweat.

To be clear, *no sweat disagreements* are real disagreements. When we elect to "agree to disagree," or move on from an unresolved dispute, we are not saying that nobody's view is right, that it's all relative, that everything is "just a matter of opinion," that arguments are pointless, or any such thing. We may hold firm to the correctness of our view, while admitting that those who disagree are mistaken rather than craven, stupid, or wicked. It's not that we don't care about the matter in dispute. In taking such a stance, we are simply recognizing that life is short, that certain questions are difficult to settle, and that we must go on despite our disagreement. Sometimes we decide to move on from an unresolved disagreement precisely for the purpose of gathering more evidence or developing new arguments in favor of our views. We table the dispute for the moment for the sake of reopening it at a later time. Sometimes we simply move on, resolving never to revisit the issue.

No sweat disagreement is a familiar phenomenon. Many healthy friendships and marriages feature such unresolved disputes; in fact, many longstanding relationships seem to be based on ongoing no sweat disagreements. Perhaps the defining characteristic of no sweat disagreement is that the matter in dispute is relatively minor . Alfred and Betty's disputes about paintings and quarterbacks are, in the grand scheme of things, of small consequence. This is not to say that they do not argue passionately, or that the question of who is the best quarterback doesn't matter to them. Of course it matters to them. If it didn't, they wouldn't bother to argue about it. We say that the dispute is of relatively minor import because what one believes about paintings and quarterbacks typically has little impact on the rest of one's life. Nothing about their disagreement prevents Alfred and Betty from being good friends, kind neighbors, or responsible citizens. They may frequent different museums and root for different football teams on Sundays. But even the most ardent fans of art and football will concede these differences don't make much of a difference overall.

Yet not all disagreements are of the no sweat variety. In some cases, lack of agreement strikes us as deeply troubling or unacceptable, and we feel that we cannot simply table the dispute. That is, sometimes people disagree about matters of such magnitude and impact that they cannot simply let the dispute go unresolved. Let's call such disputes *momentous*. When disagreement is *momentous*, those with whom we disagree seem to be not only our opponents in argument but our overall *adversaries*. We see them not simply as mistaken about the matter at hand; the fact that they disagree bothers us, it seems to be evidence of some deep failing. This is because when a disagreement is *momentous*, it concerns matters that loom large in the lives of the disputants. Again, the distinction between no sweat and momentous disputes is not that the former concern things that don't really matter to us while the latter involve things that do. We rarely bother to argue about things that don't matter to us. Instead, the difference is that in momentous disagreements, what is in dispute is something that matters to how we live our lives. In momentous disagreements, we are disagreeing about matters that are not only important but also significant to the rest of our lives.

Let us try to be more explicit. Some beliefs are central to our lives. We invest our lives in the truth of these beliefs, we live by them, and we build our lives around them. Let's call these *core beliefs*. Consequently, changing a core belief would typically cause much of one's life to change. One would have to live differently from how one lived before. These core beliefs hence are like the foundation of a house. They provide the basis upon which almost everything else rests. If the foundation is removed, the house crumbles. Similarly, when one core belief is unsettled or uprooted, we must rebuild our lives. So there is an understandable tendency to seek to preserve the beliefs that most directly inform our lives. After all, it matters how we live. Consequently, it matters what our core beliefs say about how we should live.

Our beliefs about politics and religion—we should add here beliefs about values and morality—are commonly at the core of our lives. When one's view about the artistic merits of Scorsese's films changes, we say that one has merely changed one's mind. But when one's religious, moral, or political views change significantly, we employ stronger language to describe what has happened. For example, one doesn't merely *change one's mind* about whether Jesus was divine—one *converts* to Christianity. When one comes to believe that animals have moral standing that obliges us to not eat them, one does not simply *come to agree* with the vegetarians, one *becomes* a vegetarian. Consequently, when one challenges the core beliefs of others, one thereby calls into question not merely what they believe, but *who they are.*

In short, disagreements concerning core beliefs can be *personal.* Discussion of such personal matters is usually out of place among strangers, or even acquaintances. Hence discussion of core beliefs—such as beliefs about religion and politics—is inappropriate in mixed company. Alas, it seems that Mom was right. So why are we writing this book?

II. CARING ABOUT TRUTH

We have put a lot of effort into clarifying what is correct in Mom's Maxim. But our effort to vindicate the maxim has revealed something strikingly peculiar about it as well. Recall that the reason we should avoid discussion of religion and politics in mixed company is that our beliefs about these topics are momentous. *They matter.* They guide the rest of our lives. We *live by* our beliefs about religion, morality, and politics. These beliefs tell us how we *should live.* As we've said, this is why disputes about such matters are often so *personal.* But this is also why it is important to try to believe what's *true* about these topics. Could there be a worse condition than that of the person who lives according to *false* views concerning how one should live? We all want to live well, to lead good lives, and this requires some degree of success in believing what's true about how we should live. Accordingly, not only do we want to be firm in our beliefs; we want our firmness to derive from the correctness of what we believe. Not only do we want to be unshaken; we want our core beliefs to be *unshakable.* Not only do we want to continue believing what we currently believe; we want to be able to regard our current beliefs as *worth* believing. In short, we want to believe what is *true* about religion, morality, and politics.

The aim to believe what is true about momentous matters points to something fishy about Mom's Maxim. It is no doubt important to be polite, especially in our dealings with strangers. But it is more important to believe what's true about how to live. And if we want the truth, we should want to talk with people with whom we disagree. We should want to examine the reasons they offer in support of their views; we should want to know, and even grapple with, the criticisms they have of ours. We should want to try to respond to those criticisms, and to develop our own criticisms of the opposing views. In other words, we should *care* about the truth of our religious, moral, and political beliefs. And caring about the truth of our beliefs requires us to take seriously the reasons, arguments, and criticisms of those who disagree.

Let's pause briefly at this point to attend to a likely reaction to what we have said so far. Many readers will find our talk about reasons and evidence strikingly out of place when it comes to their religious beliefs. What is distinctive about religious beliefs, they will say, is that, unlike beliefs about other matters, one holds one's religious beliefs on the basis of *faith* and not reason or evidence. More sophisticated versions of the thought hold that one's faith *is* one's evidence. Others hold that the evidence for religious belief is thus not shareable but lies wholly *within* the believer. And some will point to their *lack of evidence* as a kind of *support* for their belief. In any of these cases, it is having *faith* that is crucial for religious belief. Having reasons and evidence doesn't matter. Our call for engagement with others' reasons therefore seems irrelevant.

The appeal to faith is interesting, especially because it is unclear exactly what it comes to. As we mentioned above, sometimes faith is offered as an alternative to evidence and reasons as a basis for belief. Other times, faith is presented as a kind of evidence. But most often, the appeal to faith is employed as a way of signaling one's unwillingness to subject one's religious beliefs to the scrutiny of others. It's the more polite equivalent of saying, "Back off!"

But we need not get embroiled in the question of what appeals to faith mean. If one holds that religious beliefs are not a matter of evidence but of faith, one must give reasons for *that* belief. More generally, whatever one's particular view of the role or nature of faith is, one does not hold *that* view as a matter of faith; rather, one thinks one has *good reason* to hold that view of faith rather than some other. Furthermore, it seems to us that one's view about the nature of faith should be counted among religious believers' *religious* beliefs. Even those who appeal to faith have at least one religious belief (namely, their belief about the nature of faith) that is not itself held as a matter of faith but is based on reasons and evidence. So our call for engagement with the reasons and evidence of those with whom one disagrees is not out of place, even for those who regard certain of their religious beliefs as not subject to rational evaluation.

Let's return to the main thread. It is important to stress that taking seriously the arguments and criticisms of those with whom we disagree does not require us to adopt the attitude that our own beliefs might be false or possibly in need of repair. We are not advocating skepticism about our momentous beliefs. Neither do we advocate a wishy-washy relativism in which objections, reasons, and arguments are treated as merely expres-

sions of different "points of view" with no critical edge. R
claim is that we should take seriously those who disa
because we care about the *truth* of our own beliefs. We are inclined to say
that those who follow Mom's Maxim always and everywhere show an
inappropriately low level of concern for their beliefs. Why?

You're probably familiar with the following phenomenon. It is
known as *semantic saturation*. This is what happens when one repeats a
word out loud over and over again. (If you're not familiar with this phenomenon, try it—stop reading and spend a few minutes saying the word
box out loud to yourself.) Eventually one loses one's sense of the *meaning*
of the word one is uttering. The word's meaning fades away, and all one
hears is the sound of the word, or rather the noise one makes in uttering
it. Beliefs can be like this. When we grow accustomed to hearing only
our own beliefs, we tend to lose sight of what they mean. They become
slogans, catchphrases, dogmas, clichés, and mantras. We habitually recite
them, but they eventually lose their meaning, and we grow detached
from them. They become mere *sounds*.

By bringing our beliefs into contrast with the beliefs of those with
whom we disagree, we force ourselves to stay connected to our beliefs.
We remind ourselves of where we stand. Perhaps more important, when
we take seriously those who disagree, we bring into focus the reasons we
have for our beliefs. And this, in turn, helps us perceive more accurately
the ways our beliefs are interrelated, how they hang together, and how
they form a system of beliefs. We are therefore better positioned to see
new implications of our beliefs, new connections between what we
already believe, and new ideas that we have not yet considered. We learn;
we integrate. We are also prompted to devise new reasons and arguments
in support of our beliefs. Furthermore, we come to better understand
the views of others and thus become better able to diagnose where they
go wrong. Put simply, by engaging with those who disagree with us, we

can gain a better command of our own beliefs. We come to *be in possession* of our beliefs. By engaging in disagreement with others, we come to *know* what we believe, so to speak. If we care about our beliefs, we should seek out intelligent opposition to them. We should discuss them in mixed company. Sorry, Mom.

Now, of course, there are risks inherent in the practice of arguing about important matters in mixed company. Sometimes when we take seriously those with whom we disagree, we discover that our reasons are not as compelling as we had thought. We may also discover that there is more that can be said in support of the opposing views than we expected. We might be presented with ideas and objections we had never considered. We might find that some criticism that we had taken to be fatal to an opposing view is in fact easily defused. And we might discover that our beliefs are just false. In any of these cases, we will have to reconsider, reformulate, reevaluate, reconfigure, or revise our own views. As we have already mentioned, the experience of revising one's core beliefs can be disconcerting, frustrating, and even painful. We do not like having to admit, even if only to ourselves, that we are wrong. Nor do we like losing arguments or being bested in a debate, especially in mixed company.

These risks are significant. But, like all assessments of risk, the matter must be considered comparatively against the risks associated with alternative courses of action. We already have said that beliefs about religion, morality, and politics matter because they have a great impact on how we live our lives. How we live matters. This means that it's important to believe what's true about religion, morality, and politics. The stakes are high. Hence the risk of frustration, disappointment, and discomfort seems worth incurring, given the alternative.

Each of us lives according to some set of beliefs about how one ought to live, what is of value, what is worthy of pursuit, what our obligations are, and what is to be avoided or shunned. For most, these beliefs are formulated in the language of religion. In calling for discussion in mixed company about religious beliefs, we are not pressing a case for what is variously called "open-mindedness" or "mutual understanding." We are not calling for a celebration of the diversity of religious beliefs. We are not arguing that one owes it to others to learn about their perspectives. Of course, these may all be good things. A society of open-minded people who appreciate the diversity of religious belief and treat each other with respect is probably a society worth striving for. But we're not at present talking about what would be socially beneficial. Instead we are arguing that there is a *cognitive* requirement that calls us to engage with others about important matters. We are claiming that engaging in discussion about momentous topics in mixed company is necessary if we are to exhibit the proper care for the truth of our beliefs. Violating Mom's Maxim, and engaging with those who disagree with us, is a demand of responsible believing.

Of course, this does not mean that one must *always* be engaged in argument, or that one can *never* discuss common beliefs with friends and others. Indeed, there are contexts in which discussion of religion, morality, and politics is out of place and should be avoided. Similarly, there are contexts in which it is most appropriate to talk about momentous matters only with those who are inclined to agree. But none of these concessions amounts to an endorsement of Mom's Maxim, for it requires us to *always* avoid discussion of religion, morality, and politics in mixed company. This is a cognitively irresponsible policy. And Mom raised us to be responsible.

III. THE DARK SIDE

Mom's Maxim bids us to avoid certain kinds of conversations. It does not tell us what we should discuss in mixed company. And it does not suggest that we should avoid discussion of religion and politics in unmixed company. The point about unmixed company is crucial. Since our religious and political beliefs are so important, one should expect that people would want to discuss them with others. Following Mom's Maxim, they will discuss them only with those who are likely to agree with what they say. There are many institutions—clubs, associations, cliques, groups, congregations, parishes, networks, Internet sites, and so on—devoted precisely to helping like-minded individuals gather and communicate with each other about their common beliefs. Again, we have no objection to groups of like-minded people getting together to talk about what they have in common. Mom's Maxim, however, proposes that we should talk about religion and politics *only* with those who will agree with what we say. We argued above that this is a bad policy, that Mom's Maxim runs afoul of principles of responsible believing. Now we want to argue that the maxim has a positively dark side. It not only discourages responsible believing but also actually encourages irresponsibility with respect to belief.

We already mentioned some of the risks associated with taking seriously the views of those with whom we disagree. These risks provide a strong inclination to avoid debates in mixed company. Yet there's something so manifestly correct about the idea that responsible believing requires engagement with the opposition that we often feel compelled to say *something* about those who disagree with us. No one who is fully committed to his beliefs can avoid this. At the very least, one must hold that those who disagree are in some way *mistaken*. We are driven, in other words, toward taking account of opposing views, especially in the case of momentous beliefs. This is why so many would count among their religious beliefs their beliefs about *other* religions. Think of Catholics and Protestants. Each group has their own set of theological beliefs, but each group also has beliefs about the *other group's beliefs* as well. It is *part of each religion* to think that the other religion is in some way mistaken. This is even more obviously the case in politics. In the United States, popular political commentators tend to spend more time describing *their opposition* (mostly in highly negative ways) than affirming their positive views about policy. In the United States, part of what it is to be a Republican or a Democrat is to have a low opinion of the platform and members of the other party. When we take up momentous beliefs, we not only affirm some view about how we should live; we also adopt beliefs about others' beliefs.

It is important to get our beliefs about others' beliefs right. But, to repeat, there is a strong incentive to avoid the risks of actually engaging with those with whom we disagree. One common way of trying to avoid the risks that follow from the demands of responsible believing is to try to convince ourselves that we've already met those demands. We tell ourselves that we've already engaged with those who disagree and overcome their objections. Most commonly, we tell ourselves that our opponents really have no objections anyway; we portray them to ourselves as simply benighted, ignorant, unintelligent, lost, blind, wicked, stupid, deluded, or worse.

This tactic dominates popular political commentary in the United States. On almost any issue, the pundit's principal argument for his or her favored view is that the opposition is not simply *wrong*, but *ignorant*, *idiotic*, and *depraved*. A quick stroll through the Politics or Current Events section of any bookstore—or a cursory scan of political talk-radio and television—will confirm this. To mention only a few examples, conservatives tell us that that liberalism is a mental disorder that afflicts people who are brainless idiots. The popular liberal commentators portray conservatives as greedy liars, fools, and hypocrites who make only noise and oppose science. (We are not making this stuff up. Go to a bookstore and check the titles of recent books of political commentary.) The key to popular politics, it seems, is to hold one's opponents in contempt.

This strategy represents one simple and effective way of seeming to satisfy the demands of responsible believing while avoiding the risks of engagement. It is in fact a popular rhetorical tactic. Let's call it the *No Reasonable Opposition* strategy. It runs as follows: You tell yourself, or surround yourself with people who tell you, that there is *no reasonable opponent* to your views, that all opposition is woefully uninformed, ignorant, or irrational. If there is no reasonable opposition to what you believe, then there's no point in trying to argue with those who disagree with you. Indeed, those who disagree with you are not even worth speaking to; that they disagree shows they're stupid, deluded, or worse. Hence, there can be nothing wrong about declining to engage with them. Where there's no reasonable opposition, Mom's Maxim wins the day. The correct policy is to talk about momentous matters with only those who will agree with what you say.

As we've said, the No Reasonable Opposition strategy is a compelling and effective way of seeming to have satisfied the demands of responsible believing while avoiding the risks of engagement. But it's simpleminded, confused, and ultimately dangerous. We will take up these three charges in order.

It would be a nice world if, on every important question, there were but one obviously correct answer and a brood of other answers so obviously incorrect that only the stupid or depraved could adopt them. Were this how things are, our only problem would be that of putting the people who know the obvious truth in charge and keeping the dummies out of the way. Alas, the world we live in is much more complicated than that. Questions concerning religion, morality, and politics are so controversial precisely because they're so difficult. On almost every central question in these areas, one can find substantial disagreement among people who are not ignorant or benighted or wicked. Put otherwise, on almost every major question of religion, morality, and politics, it is possible to find informed disagreement, that is, disagreement among intelligent, honest, and sincere persons who are roughly equally informed of the relevant facts. This is due to the complexity of these issues. Often the evidence that can be brought to bear on any of these topics is itself multifaceted and complicated. Sometimes it's difficult to sort out the question of what counts as evidence, and sometimes these questions invoke subtle controversies about how different kinds of evidence are to be weighed.

To see that this is the case, take up any ongoing debate over public policy, such as the death penalty, gun control, euthanasia, or stem cell research. For those who have a weak stomach for this kind of thing, consider controversies that are less heavy, such as the permissibility of performance-enhancing drugs in professional sports, the utility of school vouchers, or the nature of intellectual property. Just choose an issue and look at the academic literature focused on it. In any of these cases, one can easily find informed and intelligent opinion on many sides. For nearly every view, there are many reasonable opponents. The No Reasonable Opposition strategy encourages us to think that with regard to the most important and perennial questions human beings can ask, there is but one simple and obvious answer, and every other proposed answer is demonstrably irrational, ignorant, or stupid. The No Reasonable Opposition strategy is for this reason simpleminded.

We hasten to emphasize that nothing in what we have just said should be taken as an endorsement of relativism. Our point has not been that since questions of religion, morality, and politics are difficult, all views are hence equally true. There's a tendency, understandable but ultimately misguided, to equate the recognition of the complexity of these issues with a "who's to say?" variety relativism. This "who's to say?" view mistakenly infers from the fact of the complexity of these matters, and the persistence of disagreement concerning them, the conclusion that everyone's opinion is somehow correct, or at least just as good as anyone else's. But "who's to say?" relativism view is clearly confused. That a group of well-intentioned, intelligent, and well-informed physicians disagree about the proper diagnosis of a given patient does not entail that the patient is not sick. That two detectives disagree about the proper interpretation of their evidence does not entail that no one committed the murder. That well-informed, sincere, and intelligent people have different beliefs about religion, morality, and politics does not entail that no one's right.

To make sense of this, we need to introduce a distinction between the *truth* of a belief and the *justification* one has in believing it. The former is simple enough to get a hold of, at least for our purposes. A belief is true when it says something about the way the world is, and the world is that way. Here's a simple example. As a matter of fact, Harrison Ford majored in philosophy in college. This means that the belief that Harrison Ford majored in philosophy in college is true. The belief claims that something is the case that, as it turns out, *is* the case; thus the belief is true. Anyone who believes that Ford majored in philosophy thus has at least one true belief. Now, imagine that our friend Abby believes that Harrison Ford majored in philosophy in college, but she holds that belief because, in the movie *Star Wars*, the character Han Solo (played by Ford) seems to say many philosophical things. Abby has a true belief. But her belief is not properly grounded. The fact that Ford once played a character who seems to say many philosophical things is not a *good* reason to believe that Ford majored in philosophy. Consider that actors most often do not write the scripts for the films in which they perform, and we know in this case that Ford did not write Han Solo's lines. We also know that other characters in that film seem to say philosophical things, and the actors who portray those characters did not major in philosophy. We could go on. In short, Abby's reason for her belief does not point to the truth of the belief; her stated reason does not really provide evidence for her belief. Abby has a true belief, but she is not *justified* in her belief.

To get a better feel for the distinction, compare Abby with Bill. Bill believes that Harrison Ford majored in philosophy in college; Bill believes this because he recently read Ford's autobiography in which Ford claims to have majored in philosophy. That Ford claims to have majored in philosophy in college provides *evidence* that he did. Thus, Bill's reason for his belief is appropriately hooked up with what he believes.

Of course, Harrison Ford could be lying in his autobiography. Or maybe the part of his autobiography in which he claims to have majored in philosophy contains a typographical error, and he actually majored in psychology. Or maybe Ford is misremembering. Or maybe Ford has been tricked into believing that he majored in philosophy. In any case, if it's *false* that Ford majored in philosophy in college, then it's clearly the case that Bill cannot *know* that Ford majored in philosophy. To have knowledge is, among other things, to have a belief that is true. One necessarily fails to have knowledge if one believes what is false. Note that one can have knowledge that some belief is false. But that's a different point from the one we're making. Here we're claiming simply that one component of knowledge is true belief; one can *know* that Harrison Ford majored in philosophy only if it's *true* that he did.

Philosophers have put a lot of effort over the centuries into figuring out the right way to understand the precise connections between truth, evidence, reasons, justification, and knowledge. The area of philosophy known as *epistemology* handles these issues, and epistemology has been a thriving business in philosophy at least since Plato. So we're putting many important questions about these matters to the side. But two things are central to this epistemological tradition in philosophy: you can know something only if it is true, and there is a difference between holding something to be true and having the evidence to believe it is true. The important implication of what we have said thus far is that even if it's false that Ford majored in philosophy, Bill could still be *justified* in believing that he did. Just as one can have a true belief but be unjustified, one can have a justified belief even if one believes what's false. *Justification* has to do with the way we gather, understand, and weigh the evidence that we take to support our belief. *Truth* has to do with the relation our beliefs bear to the world.

With this distinction in place, we can see how the No Reasonable Opposition strategy is not only simpleminded, but positively confused. When we find ourselves in a disagreement, we assert something that our interlocutor denies. When two people disagree, one says something is true that the other says is false. This much is obvious. Sadly, when confronted with disagreement people often turn instantly to efforts designed to make those who reject their views look silly or incompetent. As we argued above, this betrays a lack of regard for one's beliefs. When we show proper concern for our beliefs, we engage in argument not for the sake of making others look foolish but rather for the sake of better apprehending the truth. In proper argument, then, we try to exchange our evidence. We each try to get a view of the other's *reasons* for believing what we regard as false. And this requires us to look at the connection between what our interlocutor believes and what evidence she takes herself to have. That is, in disagreement, we have opposing views of what is true, and so we engage each other's *justification*; we attempt to evaluate each other's reasons.

Consequently, properly conducted argument involves a *diagnostic* endeavor. When we look to our interlocutor's reasons for his beliefs, we are attempting to explain the fact that he asserts what we deny. We are trying to *explain* the fact of our disagreement. Now, disagreement has many sources. It is often the case that disagreements arise because the two disputants are drawing from radically different sets of evidence. Sometimes disagreement arises because the evidence is indeterminate or sketchy. Sometimes a dispute about one issue is due to a deeper dispute about what evidence there is. Sometimes the disputants share the same evidence but weigh it differently. And so on. The point is that, among adults, it is rarely the case that anyone believes something that's not supported by what he or she takes to be the evidence. Accordingly, with most disputes, it is possible to rationally reconstruct the position of one's opponent: One can see that the opposing view proceeds from the opponent's conception of what the evidence is and how it is to be weighed. That is, properly conducted argument—argument aimed at getting a better grasp of the truth—is always aimed at *preserving* the reasonableness of those with whom one disagrees. When argument succeeds, then, we still will see the other as having a false belief, but we will also grasp his or her reasons, such as they are, and be able to say something about why those reasons fall short.

Once we are able to diagnose disagreements in this way, we will be unable to regard those with whom we disagree as necessarily deluded, ignorant, wicked, or benighted. We will see them as nonetheless wrong, mistaken, and in error. Perhaps we will see them as seriously mistaken and obviously in error. But we will also see how, from their perspectives, their reasons, such as they are, are supposed to support their beliefs. We will see them as *reasonable*, as fellow rational agents, who have, in ways that are identifiable and in principle remediable, made a mistake. Part of what it is to care about the truth about one's beliefs is to care about how reasonable people go wrong. This is in part the aim of argument. Perhaps it's the most important part.

Argument, once properly conceived, presupposes the crucial distinction between truth and justification that was introduced above. One way of capturing this distinction in a slogan is to say that there is a difference between being *wrong* and being *stupid*. Properly conducted argument depends on the idea that the fact that one believes what is false does not mean that one is therefore incompetent and cognitively beyond the pale. That someone believes what is false is almost never a sufficient reason to regard her as irrational or stupid, even if her belief is not only false but *obviously* so.

To put the matter in a different way, we can say that there are *two* kinds of evaluation we are engaged in when arguing. First, we are trying to get a better grasp of the truth. To do this, we are evaluating the evidence that can be brought to bear on the issue. Second, we are trying to get a better grasp of the cognitive condition of the person with whom we are disagreeing. We are trying to find out what evidence he has, how he came to believe as he does, and how (or whether) his evidence supports his belief. In the first instance, we are evaluating beliefs; in the second, we are evaluating believers.

It is this nuance that the No Reasonable Opposition strategy fails to capture. It conflates *belief evaluation* with *believer evaluation*. It infers from the fact that one believes what is false (a belief evaluation) that one is stupid (a believer evaluation). It claims that there are beliefs that are so obviously true that only the irremediably stupid and depraved could deny them, and then it cites the fact that there are, indeed, people who deny these beliefs as conclusive evidence that those people are stupid and depraved. But whether someone is stupid is not a question of what she believes, but rather of the relation between her beliefs and what she takes to be her evidence. The stupid person is someone who systematically and persistently believes against what she acknowledges as evidence, someone who cannot make the right connections between what she believes and what she *has reason to believe.* Someone with very limited access to the available evidence concerning a certain matter might, indeed, arrive at a seriously and obviously mistaken belief, but she would not therefore be stupid or irrational. But this is precisely the kind of judgment that the No Reasonable Opposition strategy encourages. It is therefore confused.

Finally, we hold that the No Reasonable Opposition strategy is dangerous. Here's why. Once the distinction between belief evaluation and believer evaluation is lost, so too is the possibility of what we have called *reasonable disagreement,* disagreement among well-intentioned, sincere, honest, and intelligent people. This should be obvious. (In fact, the whole point of the strategy is to deny the possibility of reasonable disagreement.) But it's dangerous to convince oneself that everyone who disagrees with you is *ipso facto* insincere, dishonest, ignorant, and stupid. It's obvious why. You must live with those with whom you disagree. They are your neighbors, your relatives, your acquaintances, your children, your doctors, your teachers, your co-workers, and so on. More important, in a democratic society such as ours, those with whom you disagree over monumental matters are your fellow citizens, people who are your political equals. Political equality in a democratic society means many things, but one of the most important is that political equals share equally in political power. Each citizen gets exactly one vote. Our democracy is based on the premise that reasonable disagreement is not only possible, but common; that well-intentioned, sincere, honest, and intelligent persons can nonetheless arrive at opposed positions about crucial questions; that debate over monumental issues is not a waste of time.

The No Reasonable Opposition strategy expressly denies this. It says that when it comes to the really important questions, there could be no reasonable disagreement, and thus nothing to debate. It is hard to see why someone who believes such a thing would support democratic political arrangements. If, as the No Reasonable Opposition strategy contends, there is but one reasonable view among only so many errors that are so obviously wrong that only the depraved or stupid could believe them, then why uphold a commitment to political equality? If, as certain conservative commentators allege, liberals are brainless and mentally disordered, why afford them equal power? If, as certain liberal commentators claim, conservatives are pathological liars and fools, why allow them to vote at all? The No Reasonable Opposition strategy has anti-democratic ramifications.

There's a further respect in which the No Reasonable Opposition view is dangerous. A well-established phenomenon of social dynamics shows that prolonged interaction among people who agree about some topic results in each member of the group coming to adopt a more extreme version of the belief he or she began with. That is, groups of like-minded people who discuss their common views tend to unwittingly *radicalize*—they cause each other to adopt more extreme beliefs. The phenomenon is known as *group polarization*, and it is the subject of several books written by legal scholar and political philosopher Cass Sunstein. To put the point simply, when one talks about important matters only with those who are inclined to agree, one loses control over one's belief. One comes to believe more extreme versions of one's original view. Of course, the more extreme version might be closer to the truth. We are not presupposing that the truth is always moderate. The important thing is that when a group polarizes in this way, individuals' beliefs shift toward more radical versions of their initial view. However, the shift is not occasioned by the introduction of new information or better arguments. The shift toward the extreme pole is purely a function of social dynamics; it is not rational.

Thus we see that the No Reasonable Opposition strategy is self-defeating. Its point is to insulate someone who believes the truth from having to bother with those who promote error. But in fact it helps promote its own kind of irrationality—namely, that of holding a belief that's more extreme than the evidence and reasons warrant. In its most overt instances, the No Reasonable Opposition strategy is presented as a dictate of cognitive virtue. One refuses to engage with the opposition for the sake of standing up for the truth, one declines to dignify the obviously wrongheaded opposition with a response. But this strategy actually runs counter to a proper concern for truth. It promotes error.

In short, the No Reasonable Opposition strategy is the dark side of Mom's Maxim. If we think that beliefs about religion, morality, and politics are indeed momentous—if we think that how we live our lives matters—we should care most of all to get the *truth* about these topics. As we have seen, caring about the truth is not simply a matter of holding the right beliefs. Like caring for a child or an elder, caring about the truth is an ongoing process of attending *to* our beliefs, looking after the grounds upon which they rest, grasping the best reasons that can be offered in their support. Caring about the truth of our momentous beliefs thus means caring about the reasons, evidence, and arguments of those with whom we disagree. It means taking care to get an accurate picture of what those reasons are. This requires us to discuss religion, morality, and politics in mixed company.

More important, caring about the truth requires us to acknowledge that, with respect to momentous issues, there is typically room for reasonable disagreement. That is, for almost any of our religious, moral, and political beliefs, one can find a well-informed, sincere, and intellectually honest opponent. We may say, then, that nearly every reasonable view admits of a reasonable opponent. Caring about the truth, then, requires us to reject the No Reasonable Opposition strategy and acknowledge that there are *reasonable* people who reject our momentous beliefs.

We hold, therefore, that Mom's Maxim should be dropped and replaced with an alternative principle of cognitive conduct, what we will call *Mill's Principle*. Nineteenth-century British philosopher and statesman John Stuart Mill wrote the following in his classic defense of individual liberty, *On Liberty*: "He who knows only his own side of the case knows little of that." Mill's Principle captures succinctly what we have been arguing thus far.

Before moving on, allow us to emphasize that the view we are promoting does not say that no one is stupid or that every argument is cognitively productive. Mill's Principle does not say that there are no ignorant, pigheaded, benighted, or foolish people. Surely there are. And trying to engage in a reasoned argument with such people is indeed frustrating. The point we have been urging is that it's wrong to think that one can distinguish an intelligent interlocutor from a silly one simply by finding out what he or she believes. Again, the judgment that argument with a given interlocutor is a waste of time is a *believer evaluation*, not a *belief evaluation*. And believer evaluations can be made responsibly only after one sincerely engages in argument with another. Accordingly, the judgment that a given interlocutor is stupid or beyond the pale should be a last resort, reached only after sincere attempts to have a reasonable argument.

IV. POLITENESS AND RESPECT

We have been arguing that Mom's Maxim prescribes an irresponsible policy regarding conversation in mixed company and that it should hence be replaced with Mill's Principle. But you will no doubt recall that at the beginning of this chapter, we credited the maxim for calling attention to the importance of politeness. What gives?

It is important to be polite to others, especially those with whom we disagree over momentous matters. We deny, however, that politeness requires non-engagement with respect to these topics. That is, we hold that Mom's Maxim employs a defective conception of argument, one that needs to be overcome if we are to take seriously the project of caring for the truth of our momentous beliefs.

We have already made a case for thinking that argument is not simply verbal combat; it is not aimed at making one's interlocutor look silly or foolish. One does not "win" in argument by humiliating one's interlocutor, getting "the last word," or reducing him or her to silence. Properly conceived and conducted argument aims instead at gaining a better grasp of the truth. And this involves the attempt to grasp the position of one's interlocutor, to see how his belief follows from his evidence, to identify what, precisely, has led him to deny what you assert, and so on. Earlier, we referred to this aspect of argument as its *diagnostic* function; in argument, we try not only to disprove our interlocutor's view, we also try to devise an explanation of his error. We try to show that our interlocutor's view, though mistaken, is a plausible position to take, given his evidence and the way he understands it. In properly conducted argument, then, we try to correct our interlocutor's erroneous beliefs while preserving his reasonableness. We also recognize that argument is a two-way street. Just as one tries to correct the errors of one's interlocutor, one's interlocutor tries to correct one's own views, to diagnose one's own errors, and to win reasoned agreement for his own position.

We hasten to add that this is not to say that argumentation needs always to be the calm and cordial conversation that one encounters in college seminars. Properly conducted argument can be loud, spirited, and impassioned. And often it is. Moreover, the aim of preserving our interlocutor's reasonableness does not require us to be wishy-washy, accommodating, or concessive. In argument, we strive to demonstrate the falsity of our interlocutor's position. We similarly put up the most rigorous defense of our own view. The gloves come off, so to speak. But the target of the bare-knuckle engagement is the reasons and arguments that can be offered in support of the beliefs in dispute. The aim is never to show that our interlocutor is stupid, deluded, foolish, or benighted; the aim is rather to show that he or she is wrong.

We argued that Mom's Maxim bids us to avoid discussion of religion and politics in mixed company because argument over these topics often turns personal. Now we see that *badly conducted* argument is aimed at impugning or humiliating the person. What is required, then, is not silence in mixed company over momentous matters but a more responsible conception of what argument requires of us. To be specific, argument requires us to be *respectful* of those with whom we engage.

It is common for people to claim to "respect the beliefs" of those with whom they disagree. This is often said in the heat of a disagreement as a way of lowering the temperature. But it is not clear what it means to respect a belief, especially a belief that one takes to be false. Perhaps one "respects the beliefs" of another when one recognizes the other's right to hold the beliefs he or she holds? This seems unlikely, because the arguments we're talking about rarely invoke claims about individuals' rights. It seems to us, then, that talk about "respecting the beliefs" of others is misplaced. Beliefs are not proper objects of respect (or disrespect). People are. And we respect others by treating them as fellow reasoners, as rational creatures. Passing over in silence what we take to be serious errors on the part of a fellow rational creature is disrespectful. It is to see them as unresponsive to rational considerations and impervious to good reasons. It is to patronize them.

The subtitle of this book refers to *respectful* disbelief. It should be clear now what this means. In the pages that follow, we hope to start an argument. More specifically, we hope to start an argument about religion. But we aspire to start an argument of the right kind. Our aim is not to try to convince religious believers that religious belief is silly or that the fact that they hold religious beliefs means that they're stupid. We think that religious beliefs are false and that religious believers are mistaken in their religious beliefs. We do not "respect" religious beliefs. We do, however, respect religious believers. We hold that religious believers can be intelligent, rational, and responsible, despite the falsity of their religious beliefs; in short, we hold that religious believers can be *reasonable* in the sense identified above.

Our aim is to show them that atheists, too, can be reasonable, that is, intelligent, rational, and responsible reasoners. We aim to do this by developing a moral account of atheism, a case for atheism that draws upon the same moral concern that frequently drives people to adopt religious belief. It is only once religious believers and atheists alike are prepared to regard each other as reasonable—and thus ready to show the respect that rational creatures owe to each other—that the debate over God's existence and the rationality of religious belief can commence in a way that has a chance of being profitable. In short, we aim to start a respectful argument by first giving some reasons and showing that there is a rational way forward for disagreement between atheists and religious believers.

CHAPTER TWO

WHAT ATHEISM IS

I. THE PROBLEM OF DEFINITION

We, the authors of this book, are atheists. What does this mean? A simple answer is given by the grammatical form of term *atheism* itself. Just as an *atypical occurrence* is an occurrence that is not typical, an *atheist* is one who is not a theist. To be more precise, an atheist is someone who *rejects* theism. Unfortunately, this simple answer is quite uninformative. At the very least, one would need to know what *theism* is to know what it means to reject it. And there are different conceptions of theism. On many accounts, *theism* is the name for a belief in a God of any kind. Others insist that theism is the belief in a *certain kind of* God, namely, a supernatural or transcendent God, a God that stands apart from the natural world. Still others tighten the focus further, associating theism specifically with belief in the God of the Abrahamic religions: Judaism, Christianity, and Islam. This is a God who created the natural world; who stands apart from His creation; who is all knowing, all powerful, all good; and who takes a keen interest in human conduct.

No doubt there are many additional conceptions of theism. And their differences are not merely verbal or otherwise insignificant. Indeed, a lot turns on the question of what theism is. Consider that if one adopts the first conception (the one that associates theism simply with a belief in any God whatsoever), atheists make up a tiny minority of the world's population. By contrast, if one adopts the third conception identified above (the one that defines theism as belief in the Abrahamic God), atheists are in the vast majority. For on the third conception, the major religions of the East (Hinduism, Buddhism, Taoism, and Confucianism), many of the world's folk religions, and many contemporary New Age religions are atheistic. Their practitioners are all atheists.

It might be less confusing to simply define *atheism* as the rejection of religion as such. To be sure, many contemporary atheists claim to oppose religion wholesale. One has gone so far as to assert that religion "poisons everything." Yet the claim that atheism is the rejection of religion is, again, strikingly uninformative until we are clear about what religion is. And this is even more complicated than the question of what theism is. *Religion* is a term we apply to a hodgepodge of institutions, doctrines, beliefs, rituals, practices, attitudes, and modes of social association. Consider for a moment the vast array of religions in the world. Some are intrinsically communal, others are individualistic; some involve vast hierarchies of religious officials, others are strictly personal; some involve elaborate rituals and ceremonies, others do not; some are based on established and authoritative doctrines, others are decidedly nondoctrinal; some are directly tied to longstanding traditions of theological and metaphysical thought, others reject such traditions. And so on.

The attempt to define *religion* gets more complicated when we add to these considerations the acknowledgment that many religions contain a distinction between religion proper and "false religion." That is, some religions use the term *religion* only in an honorific sense; they refuse to refer to creeds other than their own as religion. On such views, different creeds are not different religions but mere idolatry, religion in name only. Others hold the similar view that there is but one *true* religion, and all others are defective or incomplete versions of themselves. Even among the various sects of, say, Christianity or Buddhism, there are significant divides over the question of what religion is. In short, since it is not clear what *religion* is, it is not clear what a wholesale rejection of religion comes to. Consequently, the view that atheism is the rejection of religion is unsatisfactory.

Finally, consider that atheists themselves seem to disagree about what atheism is. According to some, *atheism* is the name of some very specific philosophical claim, such as that there is no God or that religious claims are false. Some hold the closely related view that atheism is the name of the view according to which religious claims are not merely false, but nonsensical, meaningless. It is more common, however, to associate atheism with broader commitments. For example, some hold that atheism is a necessary component of nihilism, the view that nothing has value, that there are no goods or evils. Others hold that atheism is intrinsically tied to a scientific worldview that attempts to understand everything, including good and evil, in strictly empirical terms. A familiar variant of this view holds that atheism is an entailment of evolutionary biology, and that human behavior (including moral behavior) is best understood in terms of evolution. Some see atheism as part of a more general stance of skepticism. Still others see atheism as an essential part of a humanist moral vision according to which people would be morally better were religion abandoned.

Several other versions of atheism are in currency, and there's no reason to try to catalogue them all. The point, again, is this: the claim that we, the authors, are atheists is remarkably uninformative. We hasten to add that the same is true for the claim that one is, for example, a Christian. Given the vast differences among the various sects of Christianity, it is not clear what one is asserting when one identifies as a Christian. One might protest and claim that to identify as a Christian is to affirm that one believes that Jesus is Lord. But this is simply to replace one uninformative statement with another. Of what, precisely, does

Jesus' Lordship consist? Different versions of Christianity differ sharply over this question. And we're off to the races again.

The point is worth emphasizing because we often overlook the fact that everyday pronouncements of this sort are uninformative. Someone claims, "I believe in God," and we take him to have told us something important about himself. But in fact he hasn't. Maybe he believes in the God of Abraham, or, alternatively, he may believe in the ancient Nordic God Thor. Or maybe by "God" he means something nonpersonal, such as nature or the laws of physics. Importantly, from the point of view of the believer in the Abrahamic God, belief in Thor, like a belief in a nonpersonal God, is not *belief in God at all*; it is, rather, belief in a *false* God, an idol, a fiction, a counterfeit. The believer in Thor may use the *same words* as the Christian in declaring his conviction, but he does not thereby state a belief that he has in common with the Christian.

But we often overlook these complications, simply filling in the details however we wish. So religious believers tend to take themselves to have something important in common with almost anyone else who identifies as religious or declares a belief in God, and they likewise take themselves to stand in the starkest opposition to anyone claiming to be an atheist. But these reflexes are out of place. Until it is determined what one means by *God, religion*, and *atheism*, it is not clear who has what in common with whom. And, as we suggested above, all these terms admit of a plethora of distinct meanings. It's a messy world.

II. ATHEISTS AND POTHOLES

Maybe the lesson to draw from all of this is that there is something wrongheaded in the very attempt to begin with a general definition of atheism. Some have picked up on this thought and said that since it designates a *lack* of belief, there is no way to identify a set of commitments distinctive of atheists, and thus no way to define atheism. On this view, atheists are like potholes. Each one is unique, and one can talk about them only by talking about the surrounding material. Atheists exist only in the *absence* of something else. More precisely, they exist only *because of* the lack of something else.

The pothole view of atheism is popular among certain religious believers, since it invites the image of the atheist as someone who is empty and for that reason perhaps dangerous, or at least to be avoided. On the pothole view, atheists simply need to be *filled in*, and if they cannot be filled in, one needs to steer clear of them. The rhetorical distance is short between the description of the atheist as empty and the description of the atheist as *empty-headed*. The view is popular also because in portraying the atheist as empty, it suggests that atheists are merely naysayers, people who *refuse* to adopt religious beliefs. The pothole view implies that atheists are empty-headed and stubborn. It is a straightforward deployment of the No Reasonable Opposition strategy. How convenient.

The pothole view is not right. It is true that atheism comes in many different varieties and there is no generic form of atheism, just as there is no generic form of theism. Yet atheism is not simply a *lack* of belief. Consider that newborn babies likely have very few, if any, beliefs, and they most certainly lack a belief in a God. But newborns are not properly regarded as atheists. This is so because atheism is the *rejection* of certain beliefs. It is not the mere *absence* of judgment about, for example, the existence of the God of the Abrahamic religions; it is, at the very least, the judgment that no such God exists. Put otherwise, atheism is not merely the *absence* of certain beliefs, but the *denial* of them. Atheists are not *nonbelievers*. They believe that certain religious beliefs are false.

We may have just hit upon a way of proceeding. Rather than search for a definition of atheism, we can begin by describing the atheism we, the authors, endorse. We can simply put our cards on the table, so to speak. So here goes.

III. PUTTING OUR CARDS ON THE TABLE

We, the authors of this book, are atheists. This means at least this much: We deny the existence of a God who is all good, all knowing, and all-powerful. We deny the existence of a God who is the transcendent creator of the natural world. We deny that there is any entity that is properly regarded as a deity. We deny that there is a being who deserves to be worshipped. We deny that there is anything that is divine. We deny that there are or ever have been prophets, persons through whom divine beings speak and act. We deny that there are books or texts that have been composed with the assistance of a God or any other divinity, and we deny that any existing book or text derives its authority from having been composed with such assistance. We deny that so-called mystical experiences reveal anything true about the world. We deny the claim that through prayer individuals can summon the assistance of divine beings. We deny the existence of supernatural persons, including angels, ghosts, spirits, and demons. We deny that there has ever been a virgin birth, a resurrection, and an assumption. We deny that there will be a Second Coming, a Rapture, and a Judgment Day. We deny that there are immortal souls. We deny that humans somehow survive their bodily death. We deny that souls are reincarnated, and we deny the doctrines of karma and transmigration; we deny that people have "past lives." We deny that there is an afterlife. We deny that there are persons who have the power to communicate with the dead. We deny that there is anything that is *sacred, holy, hallowed, damned, wicked, sacrosanct,* or *blessed* in the strict senses of those words. We deny the existence of miracles in the literal sense of that term. We deny that there are rituals that can transform bread and wine into flesh and blood. We deny that certain acts of speech are morally wrong because they are *blasphemous*, for we reject the existence of anything against which it is possible to blaspheme. We deny that there are acts that are morally wrong because they are instances of *sin*, for we reject sin as a moral category. We deny that there is a heaven and a hell, and we hold that the very idea of eternal rewards and punishments is morally repugnant. (Readers who are interested in this last claim are invited to consult appendix A.)

Yes, that's quite a catalogue of things we, the authors, deny. Someone looking to make a joke at our expense might say that we are living in denial. But this joke of course trades on two different senses of the word *denial*. We indeed deny many popular beliefs but are not therefore "living in denial." One who lives in denial is suffering from a cognitive disorder; one who is *in denial* is employing a certain strategy for dealing with something that she would rather not be the case. She denies that which she knows is true as an attempt to escape it; consequently, her denial is at the same time an affirmation of what is denied. Denial in this sense always involves a contradiction, and thus is always irrational. That's the cut of the joke.

The denial we engage in, however, is not irrational. We deny the existence of God and the rest because we believe that the best arguments support our views. This captures the other sense of denial that the joke trades on. As we mentioned above, atheists do not simply *refuse* to accept certain religious claims; atheists present *reasons* and *arguments* against them. In some cases, we reject claims simply for the reason that there is insufficient evidence in their favor. Extraordinary claims call for extraordinary proof; where such proof is lacking, the claim ordinarily ought to be rejected. In other cases, we reject claims because we have compelling reasons in favor of their negation. Hence, if someone claims that God is both supremely merciful and supremely wrathful, we have a good reason to think that there is no such God, for nothing could instantiate both of these properties to their fullest degree. And sometimes we reject claims because the arguments offered in their favor are defective or weak. For example, a street preacher once told us, the authors, that Christianity is true because the Bible is the most popular book in the history of mankind. Leaving aside the meaning of the empirical claim about the popularity of the Bible, the proposed argument is defective in that the truth of its premise (namely, that the Bible is the most popular book in the history of mankind) in no way provides evidence for its conclusion (namely, that Christianity is true). Atheism, then, is not mere naysaying or petulant skepticism; it's driven by reasons and arguments.

IV. THE ETHICS OF BELIEF

Atheism therefore involves the positive commitment to the idea that beliefs ought to be the objects of rational evaluation. This means, first, that our beliefs ought to reflect our evidence. We ought to believe what our best evidence indicates is true, we ought to deny what our best evidence indicates is false, and we ought to suspend judgment—and perhaps continue to inquire—when our best evidence is insufficiently determinate. Put in other words, our beliefs ought to be the *manifestations* of our evidence. And this means not only that our beliefs ought to be well supported by the evidence that is available; the relationship between the evidence and our beliefs ought to be manifest to us. We ought to be able to say *why* we believe the things we believe, and to see *how* our evidence supports our belief.

It is only in light of this connection between *what* we believe and *why* we believe it that our beliefs could be rationally evaluated. For, as we saw earlier, it is possible to believe what's true on the basis of bad, incomplete, or inappropriate evidence. And it is possible to believe what's false despite the fact that one has properly attended to all the available evidence. Part of rationally evaluating our beliefs is examining the relation of our beliefs to the evidence. But it also involves an examination of our conception of the evidence as well.

The commitment to the rational evaluation of our beliefs has a second implication. As we argued in the previous chapter, the rational evaluation of our own beliefs requires engagement with other people, people with whom we disagree. This is because the pursuit of truth requires us to gather evidence relevant to our beliefs, and it matters what reasonable people say in criticism of our beliefs. That reasonable people reject our beliefs can sometimes be evidence in itself. Sometimes others will have access to reasons and evidence that we have not considered. Sometimes others will be in a good position to correct our understanding of what the evidence suggests. Sometimes in responding to a criticism we gain a better grasp of our own position. And so on. The point is that engagement with our critics is a necessary component of responsible belief.

The atheism we endorse hence is driven by what might be called an *ethics of belief*. To explain: Beliefs are not inert objects we possess. We *hold* beliefs, we *grasp* them; we maintain, defend, and assert them. Believing is an activity or conduct, an element of human behavior. Accordingly, believing is evaluable in ethical terms. For example, one can behave with respect to one's beliefs in irresponsible ways; one can do wrong by adopting a belief on insufficient evidence; one can harm others by dismissing their testimony as unreliable. And so on.

At first it may seem odd to think that believing is an activity that's evaluable in ethical terms. But if we reflect a bit, we will find the idea not foreign at all. Consider the adage "Fool me once, shame on you; fool me twice, shame on me." The claim here is that that there is a kind of wrong associated with being careless in adopting beliefs, that gullibility is shameful, that one should not base one's beliefs on the say-so of someone who has proven untrustworthy in the past.

Take another example. You're at a party at a friend's house. Unfortunately, you're not feeling well. You have a severe headache, and you decide to take some medicine. But you mistakenly have left your usual headache medicine at home. So you go into your friend's medicine cabinet and empty into your hand a few pills out of a prescription drug bottle. The pills have a similar shape and color to the ones you left at home, so you take them, reasoning that these pills will have the same effect as the ones you usually take. Now, maybe the drug you have taken indeed relieves your headache, maybe not. Either way, you made an error of judgment, and even if your headache is gone and you suffer no consequences from ingesting unknown medications, you needlessly put yourself in danger. The point is that you *should know better* than to believe that similarly shaped and colored pills have the same effect.

Finally, let's consider a case modified slightly from one made famous by W. K. Clifford in his classic essay "The Ethics of Belief." You and some friends are planning a cross-country road trip in your car. For the past several weeks, you've noticed an odd grinding sound coming from the front end of the car, a sound typically associated with a seriously weakened axle. You know that, should the axle break on the trip, you and your friends will at the very least be stranded on the side of a road but could very well be involved in a serious car accident, which could hurt not only yourself and your friends but other people, too. The thought of either of these outcomes disturbs you so much that you resolve to simply ignore the grinding sound and convince yourself that everything is all right with the car. This belief comforts you, and you grow to sincerely believe that everything is OK with the axle. The day of the trip arrives, and off you go. Now let's suppose that the axle does indeed break, causing a serious car accident. You, your friends, and a family in their van are all hurt. You would be morally blameworthy for not having the axle inspected by a mechanic before embarking on the trip. That's obvious. But what should be said if the axle does not break, and the road trip concludes without incident? Are you any less blameworthy for having convinced yourself of the safety of the car? To be sure, you are not in this case blameworthy for having caused a serious car accident by your negligence. But aren't you blameworthy nonetheless for having formed a belief in an irresponsible way, for having formed a belief to which you were not entitled? By managing your beliefs inappropriately, you endanger yourself and others.

As these examples suggest, the ethics of belief we endorse has an inward-looking part and an outward-looking part. On the inward side, we behave in a cognitively responsible way when we strive to make manifest to ourselves the grounds we have for holding our beliefs and, in turn, check the appropriateness of the reasons we have for believing what we believe. Responsible believers strive to keep their cognitive houses in order, as it were. As for the outward-looking element, the ethics of belief reminds us that since believing is frequently intimately tied to other forms of conduct, our beliefs typically affect others. As the case of the road trip punctuates, irresponsible beliefs can put others at risk. Consequently, in many cases, we have a duty to show proper diligence in forming our beliefs.

Now, given that we have these responsibilities with respect to managing and gathering evidence, we have an overarching obligation to share, aggregate, and publicly evaluate the evidence we all have with regards to issues of importance. This requires that we not only have our own ducks in a row with our own evidence but also strive to know what evidence others have. In addition, we must cultivate the skills required for making our own reasons explicit, having the right critical things to say against beliefs we find false, and having defenses against criticisms of our own views. In short, we must develop the skills necessary for deliberating about important issues. We must be informed with regard to the matter, up to date on the discussion, able to devise arguments, and cognizant of the alternative positions. These are complex skills, and living up to these requirements can be pretty demanding. But take a moment and consider how strange it would be to embrace the alternative. For example, someone who thinks that he or she does not need to strive to meet these requirements would be likely say the following things:

> The weather tomorrow afternoon will be perfect for the company picnic, but I don't need to check any weather forecasts to believe that.

> Even though I've not even seen a game all season, nor have I checked the standings, I'm sure my favorite football team is leading the division.

> The Democrats have better budget proposals than the Republicans, whatever theirs are.

> I don't need to hear about the latest developments in drug treatments for my child's disease. The surgical option is best.

Imagine someone saying those things, with full confidence that he or she is right to do so. These statements are all irresponsible. The first two are about matters that, in the grand scheme of things, are of small concern. But they betray a carelessness that does not bode well for the person's general judgment. The third looks simply like political dogmatism and incuriousness. The fourth looks positively reckless. Someone who does not expend the intellectual effort required to understand the medical options in the care of a child is morally deficient. Each case represents a cognitive failure. Gathering, weighing, and deliberating about evidence is a requirement for cognitive success.

To sum up, we all agree that how we live matters. And how we live our lives is in part determined by how we govern our cognitive lives. Our cognitive lives are governed by not only *what* we believe and *why* we believe, but *how* we believe. How we believe is determined by our policies, habits, and practices concerning the formation, revision, and evaluation of our beliefs. To live well, we must conduct ourselves responsibly, and this includes conducting our cognitive lives responsibly. Responsible believing involves gathering evidence and evaluating it; seeking out reasonable opposition and eliciting the strongest counterarguments and criticisms; re-evaluating one's belief in light of those criticisms and, if necessary, revising one's belief; formulating one's own criticisms of opposing views; and responding to opponents' rejoinders to those criticisms. And all of this must be done in a way that respects one's opposition in the sense we described in the previous chapter.

The ethics of belief is demanding. It's easy to fail at cognitively responsible belief. It's easy to overestimate the strength of the evidence that favors one's beliefs, and similarly easy to disregard or degrade the strength of the counterevidence. It is easy to employ the No Reasonable Opposition strategy and begin arguing for the sake of humiliating the opposition or making them look silly. It's easy to cast those with whom we disagree as clueless dolts who aren't really worth talking to. It's easy to adopt Mom's Maxim and talk about momentous matters only with those who will confirm our beliefs. There is considerable comfort in the attitude that one's beliefs are so obviously true that no one in his right mind could deny them. But if we really care about how we live, we have to look beyond what's immediately comforting. We must care about the truth of our beliefs. And caring about the truth of our beliefs requires us to care about why we believe as we do and the ways in which we come to hold our beliefs. In short, if we care about how we live, we must attend to the ethics of belief. Yes, it's a tall order. But nobody ever said being good was easy.

V. PRESTO! ARGUMENTS

The atheism we endorse follows from our commitment to the ethics of belief just described. We think that a proper assessment of the evidence and arguments favors atheism. We think that many claims commonly regarded as distinctively and centrally religious are demonstrably false or demonstrably unsupported by the best arguments and evidence available. We think that an open and honest debate about the various claims we mentioned above (when we put our cards on the table) will come out in favor of atheism. Yet, as we have emphasized several times now, we also hold that one can be a religious believer and still be *reasonable*. What this means, again, is that, in our view, being a religious believer does not entail that one is deluded, ignorant, unintelligent, or even cognitively irresponsible; by our lights, being a religious believer simply means you're wrong.

It is not the purpose of this book to present our full case against religious belief. Our aim isn't even to present a case for the truth of atheism. Rather, we aspire to demonstrate that atheism is a *reasonable* position, a view that religious believers must recognize as one option that sincere, intelligent, and honest people could adopt after a competent and thorough examination of the evidence and arguments. If we succeed, religious believers may of course still regard atheism as false. But they will no longer be able to regard atheists as necessarily ignorant, wicked, dishonest, and benighted. They may even come to see atheists as valuable conversation partners.

Hence the success of this book does not depend on our ability to show that the standard arguments in favor of religious belief or God's existence fail. We believe they do, of course. But we also believe that some sophisticated arguments developed by professional philosophers are difficult to defeat, and that long and highly technical arguments are required to show where they go wrong. Once again, this is not our project. But we nonetheless are aware that certain religious believers take it to be *obvious* that atheism is false, because they take it to be obvious that there is a God. In fact, some religious believers will hold that the evidence in favor of God's existence is so overwhelming that no one in his or her right mind could reject it. They will hold that, in this case, the No Reasonable Opposition strategy is perfectly apt when it comes to the atheist.

Most frequently, religious believers of this stripe have what they claim are simple, direct, and utterly conclusive arguments for God's existence. These arguments share a common form. They begin with some undeniable and obvious fact, and then purport to draw from that fact alone the momentous conclusion that God exists. Since they have the feeling of a magician's performance, we will call them *Presto!* arguments. In this section, we want to respond, even if briefly, to the two most popular *Presto!* arguments for God's existence. Once again, our aim is not to refute the religious believer or to try to prove that God does not exist, but only to show that the question of whether there is a God is one over which reasonable people can disagree. That is, our aim is to show that the claim that God obviously exists is false. If there's a God, it's extremely difficult to demonstrate that there is. In other words, *Presto!* arguments for God's existence don't succeed.

One of the most frequent responses we encounter from religious believers is a *Presto!* version of what philosophers traditionally call the

Cosmological Argument for God's existence (also known as the "Argument from First Cause"). The argument runs like this: The world exists. Therefore—*Presto!*—there must be a God who caused the world to exist.

The argument purports to place the atheist in the untenable position of having either to accept God's existence or deny the existence of the world. But it does no such thing. Like all *Presto!* arguments, this argument employs an unspoken premise; in this case, the suppressed premise is the claim that everything that exists must have been brought into existence by something else. And once we make explicit the unspoken premise, we see how the argument fails. For if everything that exists must have been brought into existence by something else, then God must have been brought into existence by something else. Put otherwise, the argument derives the existence of God from the alleged need to identify a cause for the world's existence, but in doing so, it only calls attention to the need to provide a cause for God's existence. If God exists, and everything that exists was brought into existence by something else, then God was brought into existence by something else. Let's call the thing that brought God into existence *Shmod*. If Shmod caused God to exist, then God isn't ultimately the cause of the world's existence at all. And neither is Shmod, since Shmod, too, must have been caused to exist by something else. Call it *Supershmod*. And so it goes, on and on.

The typical response from religious believers to this criticism of their argument is instructive, as it reveals a common defect of *Presto!* arguments. They say that although the world needs to have been caused to exist by something else, God has *always existed*, and so His existence was not caused by something else. But this response violates the unspoken premise we identified above; it admits that something could exist without having been caused to exist. And this concession simply raises the question, if God has always existed, why couldn't the world have always existed? To put the point differently, if God exists but was not caused to exist, why couldn't the world exist without having been caused to exist?

The religious believer may want to respond by saying that *God is special*. Maybe He is, maybe not. Our point is that the argument derives whatever force it has (what we might call its *Presto!* quality) from the tacit premise that everything that exists must have been caused to exist by something else. Now it seems as if the religious believer must admit at least one exception, namely, God. But if, as the religious believer concedes, God is an exception to the principle that everything that exists has a cause for its existence, why not think that there might be other exceptions? Why not think that the world is another exception to the premise? The religious believer needs to answer this question. If it is admitted that the world could exist without having been brought into existence by something else, then the proposed argument for God's existence fails, for it depends upon the premise that there *must* be something that caused the world to exist.

To put the matter differently, the religious believer who promotes the argument we have been considering must claim that *God—and God alone—is special*, that God is the *only* exception to the claim that everything that exists must have been caused to exist by something else. So now the issue is why. *Why* is God the sole exception? Why *couldn't* the world have always existed? It is important to notice that we are not here asserting that the world has, in fact, always existed. We are not proposing any account of how the world came to be, if it came to be. Our point has been to show that the argument under consideration, though popular and seemingly compelling, in fact does not succeed. This *Presto!* argument has lost its magic.

We turn next to a second popular *Presto!* argument for God's existence, one that begins not from the fact that the world exists, but from the fact that the things in the world seem to be nicely put together. Philosophers since the Ancient Greeks have proposed what is traditionally called the *Teleological Argument* for God's existence (sometimes called the "argument from design"), and many advocates of the antievolution movement known as "intelligent design" employ it frequently. In its *Presto!* version, it runs as follows: The world exhibits a distinctive orderliness. Therefore— *Presto!*—there must be a God who designed the world.

The orderliness proponents of this argument have in mind varies from the complexity of the vital organs of living creatures, to the law-governed behavior of atoms, and to the harmonious structure of the solar system. Perhaps the most popular version rehearses the form of the argument first proposed by William Paley in the eighteenth century. Paley argued that, in light of the complexity and orderliness of the world, denying the existence of God is analogous to finding a watch on a deserted beach and yet denying the existence of watchmakers. Paley's version of the argument has attracted a lot of attention, and we think that David Hume's reply to Paley (in Hume's classic *Dialogues Concerning Natural Religion*) suffices to undermine Paley's version of the argument. But remember, here we're focused on the *Presto!* argument, not the sophisticated versions developed by professional philosophers and theologians.

The Teleological Argument attempts to force the atheist either to say something absurd or to admit God's existence. The purportedly absurd claim is that there could be complexity, order, and design without a designer. In fact, like the argument considered previously, the Teleological Argument relies upon the unspoken premise that there could be no orderly complexity except by design. Now, we happen to think that the suppressed premise in this case is simply false. Evolutionary theory shows us how ordered complexity could arise from blind and near-random processes. But we needn't engage the argument concerning the truth of the unspoken premise, because—like the previous *Presto!* argument—the suppressed premise, if true, undermines the force of the proposed argument.

Let's grant, for argument's sake, that it's true that there could be no entity that is both orderly and complex without it having been *designed* to be as such. Let's suppose, that is, that there is no design without a designer. We note next that, according to the religious believer, God must be orderly and complex. Designing the world was no small feat—some say it took God several *days* to do it, and God is, well, *God!* In fact, He apparently even needed to *rest* after the job was done. We can hardly imagine the effort that was required if even God found it taxing. So God must Himself be a complex entity.

And this is where the unspoken premise of the argument raises trouble for the religious believer. If God is complex, and complexity requires a designer, then God was designed. And so we're back to Shmod. Shmod designed God. But then Supershmod designed Shmod. And off we go.

Again, the proponent of this argument will want to claim that *God is special.* Unlike the complex and orderly objects in the world, God can be complex and orderly without having been designed to be as such. God is the exception to the unspoken premise of the argument. Yet, as we saw above, the proponent is actually committed to the idea that God is the *only* exception to the unspoken premise of the argument. And we simply ask why. If God is a complex and orderly entity that exists but is not the product of a designer, why couldn't worldly design also be designerless? What makes God special? Why couldn't other things be special in that way as well? The argument derived its force from the perhaps intuitive but nonetheless unspoken premise that complex things exist only because of the agency of a designer. But the argument depends upon the tacit recognition that there could be a complex thing that is not the product of design. In fact, the argument relies on the claim that God, arguably the *most* orderly and complex thing there is on the religious believer's view, was not designed. This *Presto!* argument is mere sleight-of-hand. It derives its force from a premise it ultimately, but very quietly, denies.

Let us emphasize once more that we do not claim that the foregoing considerations constitute anything like a knockdown refutation of the Cosmological and Teleological Arguments. What we claim to have shown is that the *Presto!* versions of these arguments are nonstarters. They are often presented as quick and decisive demonstrations of how atheists are silly, irrational, or ignorant, but in fact they're simple cases of careless reasoning. The overall lesson about *Presto!* arguments is clear. In order to mount an even minimally plausible argument in favor of God's existence, one would have to address deep and technical questions about causation, eternity, creation, the nature of God, the nature of the world, and much else besides. That is, to make a plausible case for God's existence, one must get serious about philosophy. But once one gets serious about philosophy one finds that, when it comes to momentous issues such as God and religion, there are no simple arguments or short answers.

VI. MYSTERIANISM AND THE UNKNOWN

Presto! arguments have the virtue of at least implicitly accepting the ethics of belief that we described earlier. Proponents of *Presto!* arguments begin from readily available and widely shared facts, such as that the world exists, or that the human eye is a complex mechanism. They then propose that God's existence is required if we are to make sense of these facts. Those who propose *Presto!* arguments are typically driven by the thought that we ought to strive to explain the world around us and adopt what beliefs arise out of that effort. So far, so good. The claim of the proponent of a *Presto!* argument is that God's existence is *necessary* if we are to explain our world, that God plays an essential explanatory role in our cognitive lives. Again, so far, so good. We, the authors, dispute the explanatory necessity of God and are ready to take up the argument. As we showed above, the *Presto!* arguments begin by evoking claims about what needs explanation and what could count as an explanation that are later quietly abandoned. This seems to us a straightforward error about how arguments work and what an explanation is. And we're ready to hear from the religious believer a response about these matters.

But here things typically go off the rails. The problem with *Presto!* arguments, and many of the more serious arguments for God's existence, is that they inevitably dissolve into what we will call *mysterianism*. When one says *God is special*, one is frequently simply asserting that the philosophical buck stops with God; He is the explanation for everything but is intrinsically mysterious, unspeakable, ineffable, and hidden.

This is an odd stance to take in the context of what is supposed to be an argument *in favor of* God's existence. Where God's existence is precisely what's at issue, one scores no philosophical points by simply asserting that God is what explains everything, full stop. Unless one is able to say something more about why, for example, God—and only God—exists without need of a prior cause, the appeal to God as the cause of the world's existence accomplishes no real explanatory work. If you say that the world needs to have been caused to exist because it would be absurd to say otherwise, and then go on to assert that God is the cause of the world's existence, you've told me nothing about how the world came to be or why. You've not only explained nothing at all, you've said nothing that could count as a reason for anyone to adopt a belief in God. You've merely asserted that God, though intrinsically mysterious and unexplainable, is the ultimate explanation for everything.

Atheists are frequently portrayed as arrogant smarty-pants wiseacres who can't bear to admit that there's something they do not know. They are presented as people who hate mystery and wonder, clinging close-mindedly to only the cold, hard facts. But we think that this depiction, though popular, is entirely backward. To invoke God as the answer to

Big Questions of the universe, but then say that God is intrinsically mysterious, is really to assert that those questions are *unanswerable*. And when we take Big Questions about, for example, the nature of the universe and the purpose of life to be unanswerable (because all one can say in response to them is the word *God*), we have no reason to look for more informative responses to those questions. More important, we have no reason to inquire or investigate together, and no reason to examine each other's ideas. Put simply, to invoke God in these contexts is to shut down the quest for wisdom. It is to close off the mystery by asserting that answers to the Big Questions are *unknowable*.

It is *this* that the atheist denies. We, the authors, are more than comfortable with the thought that there is much of importance that we do not know. Yet we reject the thought that progress is impossible. By our lights, it is the religious believer who denies the mystery of existence, for it is the religious believer who tends to think he or she has the explanation for everything, namely, God; and it is the religious believer who tends to hold that, since God is ultimately unexplainable and intrinsically mysterious, God is really no mystery at all.

VII. ATHEISM AND MORALITY

Let's return now to the description we gave earlier of the kind of atheism we, the authors, endorse. Recall that we presented a long list of statements about what we deny. We hope that one feature of that list caught your eye: the final few items on the list invoked decidedly *moral* judgments. To be specific, we denied that certain acts of speech are morally wrong because they are blasphemous; we denied that there are acts that are morally wrong due to their being instances of sin; and we affirmed that the idea of eternal rewards and punishments is morally repugnant.

These claims might have seemed noteworthy to some readers because according to popular views, atheism is an *amoralist* view. That is, it is popularly held that atheists must reject the very idea of moral evaluation, that they must replace the categories of *good* and *evil* with something else, such as *legal* and *illegal, interest-serving* and *interest-defeating*, or *approved of* and *disapproved of.* The popular view, in short, holds that only religious believers can recognize that there are goods and evils in the world. Accordingly, the popular view also contends that since atheists cannot recognize good and evil, they are not capable of being good and hence are evil.

The foregoing discussion of the ethics of belief should have signaled that we, the authors, recognize objective goods and evils and are willing to regard certain practices as objectively irresponsible, blameworthy, laudable, and so on. That is, we reject the popular image of atheism as an *amoralist* view. In fact, we hold that atheism not only is capable of recognizing and honoring all the standard categories of moral evaluation but is in fact often the *product* or *result* of taking those categories seriously. In other words, we think that many of the main considerations in favor of atheism are *moral considerations*. Moreover, we hold that the most philosophically compelling accounts of the nature of good and evil make no reference to (and are not in need of) God or any other religious consideration. We think that not only is it possible to be good without God, our best understandings of the nature of morality have no need of Him.

In coming chapters, we will take you through a tour of nonreligious moral theory. We will examine and evaluate several theories. Again, our task is not to prove that some nonreligious account of morality is correct. The task is rather to show that it is possible for atheists to accept many moral commitments that religious believers endorse. Atheists can believe in objective good and evil, they can condemn torture, they can fight for justice, they can honor promises, they can be kind, they can be altruistic, they can honor virtue and disparage vice, and so on. And they can provide an account of all these commitments without mentioning or invoking God. In other words, the aim is to show that the difference between atheists and religious believers is not necessarily a *moral* difference.

Before embarking on this path, though, we need to say something about how our views compare with those promoted by a series of recent writers who are commonly referred to as *The New Atheists*.

CHAPTER THREE

ON THE NEW ATHEISM

The view that atheists are immoral and stupid goes back to at least the Old Testament. Consider the Psalmist:

> The fool hath said in his heart, There is no God. Corrupt are they, and have done abominable iniquity: there is none that doeth good.... Every one of them is gone back: they are altogether become filthy; there is none that doeth good, no, not one. Have the workers of iniquity no knowledge? Who eat up my people as they eat bread: they have not called upon God.... God hath scattered the bones of him that encampeth against thee: thou hast put them to shame, because God hath despised them. (Psalm 53: 1–5)

The Psalmist affirms that those who deny God's existence are fools. And fools, according to the Psalmist, are both morally and intellectually corrupt. Consequently, according to the Psalmist, atheists deserve to be destroyed because God hates those who do not believe in Him.

A few things are worth noting about this Psalm. First, it is evident that the Psalmist knows that there are atheists. Apparently these atheists said that there is no God, and they said it not only in their hearts but out loud for others to hear. Perhaps they denied God's existence to the Psalmist himself. So atheism isn't something new; it's not a modern invention, it's not something that happened only after the time of miracles, and it's not a symptom of the fall of civilization. There were atheists even in biblical times, living among the great figures of the Bible.

Second, note the tone of the passage. The atheist, so says the Psalmist, is a *fool* who is *corrupt* and thereby deserves *contempt*, and ultimately *destruction*. This seems a straightforward employment of the No Reasonable Opposition strategy we mentioned earlier. The Psalmist fails to distinguish between *belief evaluation* and *believer evaluation*, and thus takes those whom he finds in error to be thereby evil, stupid, and worthy of little more than contempt. There is thus no need to attempt to *reason* with the atheist, to find out why he says that there is no God. In saying that there is no God, the atheist proves himself to be a fool. And fools are not worth talking to.

The Psalmist's attitude toward atheists has been very popular among the faithful for centuries. It persists even today. Consider the following. We, the authors, live in Tennessee. The Tennessee State Constitution includes a section expressly prohibiting atheists from serving in any governmental office:

> No person who denies the being of God, or a future state of rewards and punishments, shall hold any office in the civil department of this state. (Article 9, Section 2)

This prohibition is no doubt a result of the view that in denying the existence of God, atheists prove themselves to be untrustworthy, wicked, contemptible, and incapable of responsible citizenship. Consequently, even if an atheist were to win an election or prove especially well-qualified for a given position in the state government, he or she nonetheless could not serve in the office. Think of it. According to the Tennessee Constitution, atheists are unfit to issue drivers' licenses or to enforce speeding laws.

Arkansas goes even further than Tennessee. In the Arkansas Constitution, not only is it asserted that atheists are unfit to serve in government, Arkansas atheists are prohibited from testifying in court!

No person who denies the being of a God shall hold any office in the civil departments of this State, nor be competent to testify as a witness in any Court. (Article 19, Section 1)

Let's take a moment to think about this feature of the Arkansas Constitution. It's absurdly discriminatory, isn't it? And it's dangerous as well. Consider a story. Suppose that Mary is driving across the country, and she stops in Conway, Arkansas, to fill up her car with gas. As she waits for the tank to fill, she is set upon by thugs, who violently beat and rob her. Shortly after the incident, she is found by Sam, the gas station attendant, who is an atheist. Imagine that although Mary is unable to describe those who assaulted her, Sam got a decent look at the thugs as they were speeding away. However, Mary's assailants will likely not be arrested or prosecuted, simply because of Sam's legal status in Arkansas. He cannot serve as an eyewitness in court.

Imagine, for a moment, a modern-day state constitution that prohibits Christians from testifying in court, being appointed sheriff, or ever running for public office. Imagine an official state document that asserts that your word and your character are morally corrupt, not because of anything you've ever done, but simply because of your religious beliefs. Could such an arrangement possibly be just?

In our story, Sam is powerless to help Mary, and, moreover, he is powerless to help himself. If the thugs came back, and even if Sam saw their faces clearly, he would still have no legal status, and he would not be permitted to point them out in a trial. Notice that these aren't laws that were on the books in faraway lands a long time ago. These are parts of state constitutions in the United States of America in 2010! *Right now* the authors of this book are *legally prohibited* from running for public office in their home state.

One often hears in the United States these days that religious belief is under attack, and that the rights of religious believers are threatened by an encroaching public secularism. These pronouncements are driven by the sound political principle that citizens must be regarded as political equals, and no one's rights are to be determined by his or her religious commitments. We, the authors, are of course committed to equality and to freedom of conscience. We note that one rarely hears religious believers objecting to the statutes we have just discussed. Yet it is clear that a state constitution that prohibits atheists from holding positions in civil government violates their freedom of conscience and treats them as less than equal. Where is the outcry among those religious believers who claim to take freedom of conscience and political equality so seriously? How can it be sincerely maintained that religious belief is under attack in the United States when powerful legal and social sanctions against atheism persist?

It strikes us as ironic, then, that in contemporary discussions of these matters, it is the atheists who are charged with impropriety. Atheists are said to be rude, aggressive, uncivil, arrogant, and insulting. Even when they are called upon to present their views in popular forums, they are most often met with responses that ignore the substance of the atheist position, and simply express disapproval of the way in which atheists express themselves. Put in other words, the popular discussion about atheism is nearly exclusively fixed on the demeanor of the atheist. And the presumption is that openly rejecting religious belief is itself an uncivil act, and thus to be avoided. The most common way of pressing this view begins from the claim that religious believers find atheism offensive, and because they find atheism offensive, religious believers find the expression of atheistic views offensive. The next move is to confuse *offense* with *harm* and declare the atheist morally out of bounds because people generally find what he or she says harmful. Norms of public decorum require the atheist to be silent, even when invited to speak. What is the proper response to this?

I. THE QUESTION OF "TONE"

A movement widely dubbed *The New Atheism* has adopted a distinctive strategy for dealing with the ways in which atheist views are publicly dismissed. New Atheists have taken to using some pretty combative language with regard to religion and religious believers. The strategy, we think, is to vigorously assert one's right to speak frankly on behalf of one's unpopular views, and this is done by actually speaking forcefully in terms designed to shock, affront, and offend religious believers. Accordingly, journalist Christopher Hitchens has famously claimed that "religion poisons everything" and that the faithful are all too often "credulous idiots" (2007: 25; 2007: 254). Sam Harris refers to theology as "ignorance with wings" (2004: 173) and holds that religious belief is "reprehensible in its arrogance" (2006: 74). Philosopher Daniel Dennett analogizes religious beliefs to "addictions" (2006: 14) and asserts that, given the track record of religious believers, "safety demands that religions be put in cages" (1995: 515). Distinguished evolutionary theorist Richard Dawkins has said that the thought behind religious belief is "pathetic and contemptible" (2006: 285). Michel Onfray is perhaps the most direct: "Monotheism loathes intelligence" (2005: 67).

These New Atheists regularly employ the No Reasonable Opposition strategy. This quick slip, you will recall, involves the failure to distinguish being *wrong* from being *stupid*. Again, it is possible to do one's best in collecting and responding to evidence and yet still arrive at false beliefs. Thus it does not follow that those who hold false beliefs are, by the fact, irrational, incompetent, dishonest, or foolish. With respect to the most important matters, there is room for reasonable disagreement; it is possible for well-intentioned, sincere, intelligent, and knowledgeable people to come to different conclusions. The New Atheists seem to be unwilling to acknowledge this. And they have been widely criticized for taking an inappropriately aggressive tone in addressing those with whom they dis- agree. Writing for *The New Republic*, Damon Linker expresses a common sentiment; he describes their style as "hostile" and "bellicose" (2007: 16).

We made the case in our first chapter for respectful disagreement and ongoing debate among atheists and religious believers. We argued that the recognition of the possibility of reasonable disagreement requires us to engage with opponents in ways designed to bring the best arguments, reasons, and evidence to light. Hence one might expect that we would disapprove of the New Atheists. And in some ways we do. But, as we already indicated, there is another dimension to contemporary discussions of religious belief, one that complicates matters significantly. We can put the issue in the form of a question: What should one do when involved in a momentous disagreement in which it seems that one's good arguments are simply not getting through to those on the other side? What should one do when it seems as if one's opponent isn't really listening to one's arguments? What is the proper response to an interlocutor who says, "It's just a reasonable disagreement, so I can believe what I want"? When arguing an issue about which there may be reasonable disagreement, how should one respond when it seems that the other side is being unreasonable? It seems that sometimes one needs more than coolly articulated reasons and arguments. But what other means are appropriate? To put the question more pointedly, is taking a deliberately confrontational and condescending tone permitted?

II. THE PARABLE OF TOM

Let's take a step back. For a disagreement to be a *reasonable disagreement*, both sides must themselves be reasonable participants in the exchange. Both sides must present arguments, provide evidence, offer responses to the other side's criticisms, and, when appropriate, acknowledge and make concessions when criticisms succeed. Hence being reasonable requires more than simply staying calm and friendly in the midst of a serious disagreement; reasonableness is in part a *cognitive* ideal as well. To see this, consider what we'll call *The Parable of Tom*.

Imagine that you are locked in argument with someone named Tom. After you've justly criticized one of his views and his arguments for it, Tom nonetheless continues to assert his view categorically and present his arguments just as before, as though you hadn't spoken. Perhaps you may respond by pressing your objections again, or maybe you decide instead to raise new objections. But there's no change in Tom; he keeps repeating his initial view and restating the same arguments. You may even try to develop an argument that employs many premises that Tom himself employs. But Tom simply blinks and then just continues. It's almost as if you're not really there; Tom is simply *going through the motions* of argument: He is *playing* at engagement with the other side.

Now, if the issue in dispute doesn't matter much, you may be irritated by Tom's performance, but you will likely be able to let it go. That is, you may be involved in what we earlier called a *no sweat* disagreement. And part of being a grownup among other grownups is to have a healthy tolerance for the casual dogmatism of others. But let's suppose that your disagreement with Tom is not of the *no sweat* variety. Suppose the issue in question is one that has consequences for how we should conceive of our country, how we should treat others, how our children should be educated, or how we should live. Imagine, further, that Tom's view is quite popular, that Tom represents a large segment of the population of your country and perhaps the world. You recognize that there are issues about which people may reasonably disagree; it's just that you're not finding any people on the other side who seem to be doing their part. They're polite enough, but they don't respond to your arguments and objections. They respectfully listen to what you say, but simply go on, unaffected. Like Tom, they seem to merely be going through the motions. What should you do?

Of course, you could stick with your arguments. You could keep giving them, and you could continue to develop them and improve them. You could keep presenting them to Tom and the others like him. And you could keep getting ignored. Good luck with that.

Another thing you can do is *change the tone* of your presentation. You can still give the arguments, but say things that might get Tom's attention. You could call him a *doofus*, or a *credulous idiot*, or a *nincompoop*. That'll rattle him a bit; it might hurt his feelings a little, too. But it might just wake him up, or at least force Tom to get his hands dirty with real argument. It might just make him think something like: *This person just called me an idiot! I'll show her!* And then he might just respond to a criticism or two. He might just show how smart he really is by criticizing all your arguments. He might be motivated to argue *with* you, instead of repeating his mantras.

We agree that name-calling is harsh. It is warranted, if at all, only in the most extreme argumentative situations. So perhaps there are better ways to confront Tom. Maybe you could raise your voice here and there. Maybe you could turn on some sarcasm when talking about how well Tom is doing at the argument. Socrates did this. In fact, philosophers use the term *Socratic irony* to describe the tactic of praising one's interlocutor for his or her contributions to a debate when it is clear that they are not very good. Or you could just tell Tom he's not doing what he needs to be doing; you could say that he needs to respond to your criticisms, rather than continuing to repeat his talking points. (Talking points are just that: ways to keep talking, not points that facilitate discussion.) Whatever strategy you adopt for getting Tom to engage, the hope is that Tom will snap out of his broken-record routine of repeating of the same arguments and will start a real discussion. It's rude and risky, but permissible if your heart is in the right place.

But taking this confrontational route has a price. Once you adopt a strategy for shaking Tom out of his routine, you incur a correlative burden not to turn out to be like Tom yourself. Should Tom come back with new, sophisticated defenses of his views, you don't get to stick with your old criticisms. You don't get to keep calling Tom a doofus. You don't get to continue complaining about how he never pays attention to criticisms. And when Tom criticizes your arguments, you don't get to keep giving them back to him again and again. In short, if Tom turns it around and starts arguing like a reasonable person worthy of having a reasonable disagreement, you'd better do the same. A change in tone ramps up the rational standards for both sides.

The Parable of Tom helps us identify some important norms of argument. We see that tone matters in argument. However, we also see that there are circumstances in which it is appropriate to adopt a tone that is confrontational; it is even appropriate in some cases to employ various nonrational means to get an interlocutor riled up. If you don't think the other side is being an honest participant in the discussion, it is appropriate to say so. Most often, one must be polite in argument. Indeed, calm, reasoned, and respectful engagement should be the default in argumentative exchanges. But there are times when rudeness is most effective and appropriate. Importantly, the objective in these escalations in tone is not to dismiss people like Tom as ignorant and unworthy of argument, but rather to spur them to be better interlocutors. That one's intellectual opponents may hold one in contempt for one's performance should motivate one to be better. We should be free to express and communicate our frustrations when we communicate and argue. Combative tone is a good, useful thing when used properly.

But we must be careful. Escalations in tone look a lot like instances of the *ad hominem* fallacy. The fallacy of *ad hominem* argument consists in calling your opponent an idiot (or a drunk, or a fool, or anything else that comes to mind) and then concluding from this that the things the opponent says are false. What makes *ad hominem* abuse a fallacy is that it infers from the premise that someone has a particular vice that the person is wrong about the issue at hand. For example, it may be true that Richard is a drunk. That doesn't entail that his political beliefs are false. In fact, it may just be that Richard's thorough knowledge of politics has driven him to drink!

Taking an aggressive or rude tone with Tom is not to employ the *ad hominem* fallacy. When you call Tom a doofus, you are not attempting to infer from the premise that Tom is a doofus the conclusion that Tom's views are false. You adopt the confrontational language to highlight that Tom should be doing better. In other words, when you say to Tom, "Tom, stop being a blockhead and answer my question!" you are not thereby arguing fallaciously. In fact, you're not arguing at all. You are *instigating* Tom; you are trying to provoke him to take up an argument and to motivate a better performance. Tom was sleepwalking through the discussion. In calling him a blockhead, you're trying to wake him up.

III. THE TONE OF THE NEW ATHEISTS

It should be clear from what we have just said that we have no objection to the *tone* of the New Atheists. It is perfectly acceptable to call out the charlatans, liars, and dolts on the other side of an issue; indeed, it is a positive requirement that one do so. And in some cases, it is permissible that one does so with maximum prejudice. Has someone fudged the statistics? Call 'em out! Has someone tried to get away with asserting something that she knows is false? Get after her! Has someone proved himself to be ignorant of some subject matter in which he claims to be expert? He should be absolutely ashamed of himself, and he should be appropriately discredited. The New Atheists are very, very good at this. Dawkins and Dennett regularly catch and shame liars about science with great force. Hitchens and Onfray call out the immorality and hypocrisy of so many defenders of the faith with just the right amount of heat. And Harris correctly abuses the willful irrationality of so many of his opponents. When the opponent deserves it and the situation demands it, bare-knuckle confrontation is a good thing, both morally and intellectually.

But problems arise once bare-knuckle confrontation becomes the argumentative norm among disputants. We want to pick out two for discussion. First, bare-knuckle confrontation breeds outrage on all sides of a debate. And outrage is addictive. This is evident in the breathlessness with which so much of the 24-hour cable news culture works. The view seems to be that, unless there's a crisis, there's no news worth reporting. So the cable news is filled with instigations to outrage. The same goes for bookselling. We were told several times by publishers that no one wants to read a book with soberly laid out arguments about how we must respect those with whom we disagree about momentous matters. A successful book, we were told, must portray the opposition as evil, malicious, two-faced, and so on, lest readers get "confused" about the book's message.

The point is that, as debate grows confrontational and tone escalates, members of all sides become increasingly indignant and outraged by the opposition. And they want to feed their outrage, increase the degree of contempt they feel for the opposition. But when arguments are aimed not at gaining a better grasp of the truth but at confirming the disputants' low opinion of those on the other side, everyone's capacity for rational engagement suffers. Accordingly, when the New Atheists employ their confrontational tone, despite its purpose of instigating an improved mode of public discourse, they indirectly and perhaps unwittingly harm rational discourse. They become the examples to which religious believers turn when they want to paint atheists as unhinged, arrogant, and wicked. They make themselves easy targets for the No Reasonable Opposition strategy.

Now consider a second problem. Once you've gone confrontational and turned up the rhetorical heat, you must be exemplary in further exchange with the other side. Once you call Tom a blockhead or turn on the snark with one or two of your points, you've incurred the obligation to be an excellent, conscientious arguer in the subsequent discussion. In other words, one of the consequences of turning confrontational is that one's dialectical burdens increase. One who adopts the strategy of name-calling or aggressiveness thereby incurs heightened responsibility in argument. The reason is simple. It is permissible to adopt such tactics only for the sake of improving one's interlocutor's performance in the debate. But once one takes up the role of assessing the other's performance, one must prove oneself excellent in argumentation. To put the point in a different way, when one goes confrontational, one is attempting to *teach* one's interlocutor something about what good argumentation requires. But to rightfully assume the role of teacher, one must be able to prove oneself a master of that which one seeks to teach others.

This is where we think the New Atheists fall short. That is, the problem with the New Atheists is not that they are too confrontational or aggressive. We believe that their tone is often well warranted. The problem rather is that they employ the strategy of confrontation purportedly for the sake of enforcing the requirements of well-run argument, but then they fail to live up to their own argumentative burdens.

IV. THE ONTOLOGICAL ARGUMENT AND CRITICAL FAILURES OF THE NEW ATHEISM

The point is simple: If you're going to be combative, aggressive, and condescending, then you must not only bring to the debate very powerful reasons but you must also hold yourself to the highest standards of conduct in argument. Proper argument requires us to argue not only forcefully and rationally but also *honestly*. And honest argument is *fair* argument. Fair argument requires us to give our opponents their due, and this in part means that we must engage with the *best* arguments they have to offer. The New Atheists, we hold, fail to live up to this requirement. They fail to engage with the best versions of the views they criticize, electing instead to respond to the especially weak arguments commonly offered in support of religious belief. But if the aim is to expose religious belief as silly or poisonous and to call out religious believers as idiots, the New Atheists need to show that the most serious and compelling arguments for religious belief fail. It's easy to knock down weak arguments for religious belief. But there's no achievement in pinning the amateurs to the canvas. What counts is how well one can do against the pros.

We take the Ontological Argument as the litmus test for intellectual seriousness, both for atheists and religious believers alike. Anyone who takes the question of God's existence seriously must grapple with this fascinating argument. Those who simply cast it aside, or wield it indiscriminately, prove themselves intellectually careless. The debate over the merits of the Ontological Argument has raged at least since the Middle Ages. Anyone who cares about getting the truth about God's existence needs to take seriously this long-standing and ongoing debate.

In its simple form, the Ontological Argument looks like nothing more than another *Presto!* argument. Indeed, the Ontological Argument seems positively magical. The core of the argument is the claim that God, by definition, is supremely perfect. As a consequence of His supreme perfection, God is perfect in every way and lacks nothing that could make Him better. If God lacked existence, He would not be perfect, because an existing God is a better God than one that does not exist. The argument concludes that God *must* exist, because He, by definition, is supremely perfect. Here is another way to run the Ontological Argument: God, because He is supremely perfect, is the very best thing possible. Let's imagine an entity with all the relevant omniproperties (omniscience, omnipotence, and omnibenevolence). Now we ask: is it more perfect to exist only in imagination or in reality? It is better to exist in reality, so God, because He is the most perfect thing, must exist in reality, too. Therefore God exists. More important, God necessarily exists. It is impossible for Him not to.

To be sure, the Ontological Argument has the sense of being a conjuring trick or verbal sleight of hand. Calling it a linguistic trick does not explain what has gone wrong with the argument. But this is precisely the level of criticism many New Atheists muster against the Ontological Argument. They simply call it names or dismiss it as a trick. Perhaps it *is* just a trick. But one cannot simply *declare* it a mere trick and move on. One must *show* where it goes wrong. And this is notoriously difficult to do. Hence the centuries of heated debate over its merits. It is our view that good argumentative practice demands that atheists must be able to state a decent objection to the Ontological Argument, or at least give it a decent try in a discussion of it. The New Atheists don't do very well on this score. Let's look at a few examples.

Christopher Hitchens does not seem to understand the argument at all. He presents it in the following mangled form: "if god can be conceived as an idea, or stated as a predicate, he must therefore possess the quality of existence" (2007: 265). He then says the same thing can be said of *money in his pocket*. Such thoughts, he holds, are "traditional tripe" and one refutes them by "growing up" (2007: 265). But, of course, the Ontological Argument doesn't work in the way Hitchens supposes, or at least good versions of it don't. The simple version of the argument we sketched above isn't vulnerable to Hitchens' critique. Hitchens seems to hold that the Ontological Argument derives its force from the questionable premise that if a word is meaningful, it must pick out an existing object. But the Ontological Argument depends on no such premise. Rather, the argument derives God's existence from something we know about God, whether we think he exists or not, namely, that He is perfect. Now, Hitchens is no dummy. He just isn't taking the argument seriously. He hasn't bothered to engage with the more compelling forms of the argument. But *that is his job*, especially given that he has raised the standards by being intellectually confrontational.

Daniel Dennett is a distinguished philosopher, and it is not surprising that he states the Ontological Argument correctly. But his response is to analogize the perfection of God to the perfection of an ice-cream sundae:

> Could you use the same argument scheme to prove the existence of the most perfect ice-cream sundae conceivable—since if it didn't exist there would be a more perfect conceivable: namely one that *did* exist? (2006: 241)

Dennett acknowledges that one can prove the existence of certain logical objects—numbers with special mathematical properties, points with specific geometric properties, propositions with certain logical properties—in the way employed by the Ontological Argument. However, he insists "you can't prove that something that has effects in the physical world exists except by methods that are at least partly empirical" (2006: 242). Dennett holds that at best the Ontological Argument yields "a remarkably bare and featureless intentional object" (2002: 242). This is an interesting concession. But notice that Dennett seems to have ignored the core premise of the argument, namely, that God is *perfect*. And so the argument yields more than a bare or featureless object; if it yields anything, it yields a being with all perfections.

Richard Dawkins also presents the Ontological Argument accurately. But he is quick to call it "infantile" and a "mere word game"; he holds that the reasoning it employs is that of a "childish wiseacre" (2006: 80–81). Then he boasts:

> I've forgotten the details, but I once piqued a gathering of theologians and philosophers by adapting the ontological argument to prove that pigs can fly. They felt the need to resort to Modal Logic to prove that I was wrong. (2006: 84)

There are several problems with this, but we'll raise only a few things here. First, when assessing arguments—and especially when one takes oneself to be pressing crushing criticisms of long-standing arguments—*the details matter.* If Dawkins really did make the analogous argument about flying pigs, it would be useful for him to try to remember or reconstruct it for his readers. It would help us gauge Dawkins's grasp of the argument to see how he thinks the Ontological Argument can be reformulated to provide a proof that pigs can fly. But instead, all we get is just another story of confrontation without the requisite argumentation. Not a good start.

Second, Dawkins says that his audience of philosophers and theologians had to "resort to Modal Logic" to correct him. The intended conclusion is that Dawkins was not *really* corrected, but only had people respond to his claims with rules from some made-up or hocus-pocus kind of logic. But modal logic is certainly a real logic, with real rules and real regimentation that capture real requirements for thinking responsibly about possibility and necessity. Consider that any time you say that something *can't* happen, or is *possible*, or *must* be some way or other, you are making what logicians call a *modal* claim. And there are rules for how to reason about any of those claims. That's what modal logic is about. It's not made-up hooey; it attempts to track the nature of necessity and possibility. For example, if someone infers that something is *actual* from the fact that it is *possible*, that person has committed an error of reasoning. Modal logic is a tool for explaining and correcting that type of error. But Dawkins apparently thinks so very little of his opposition that he takes it to be more likely that they have made up a kind of logic to correct him than that he has made an error of reasoning. He might have taken up the challenge of showing why the modal logic employed in sophisticated versions of the Ontological Argument is dubious. But since he already knows that the argument is infantile, he feels no need to address the issue at all. This is No Reasonable Opposition strategy in spades.

To be clear, our point is that one may of course express suspicions that the Ontological Argument is more wordplay and mumbo jumbo than proof. But once one has said that the Ontological Argument fails, one must then endeavor to show how. And showing how the argument fails requires one to take up the best versions of the argument. The New Atheists effectively treat the traditional arguments for God's existence as though they were garbage. We agree with the New Atheists that they are all failures. But they are hardly garbage. In fact, exposing their flaws takes a lot of hard philosophical work. And every criticism draws responses from competent and intelligent religious philosophers. The arguments go on. But the criticisms the New Atheists have proposed gain no ground in the existing debates.

V. AN ONTOLOGICAL ARGUMENT
AGAINST GOD'S EXISTENCE

Before moving on, allow us to briefly present a criticism of the Ontological Argument that we believe lives up to the requisite argumentative burdens. Again, we do not take this to be the final word on the matter, but we think that the following line of thought is likely right. Bluntly, our claim is that *the Ontological Argument sets us on the road to atheism.* To be more dramatic, we say that we have an Ontological Argument *against* God's existence. Here goes.

We start where the traditional Ontological Argument starts, namely, with the thought that God is, by definition, supremely perfect. It is important to notice what this premise means. If you're affirming the existence of a Really Good, Really Wise, and Really Powerful entity, you're not affirming the existence of God. Similarly, if you're denying the existence of an Extremely Powerful, Good, and Wise entity, you're not denying God's existence. That seems right to us. God is good, powerful, and wise all right, but His goodness, power, and wisdom must stretch beyond our inherently limited powers of comprehension. To see this, consider that God is not simply *the best thing* there is; He is *the best possible thing.* He is not simply *the most powerful thing there is*; He is the *most powerful thing possible.* He is not simply *the wisest thing that exists*; He is the *wisest possible thing.* Once we introduce these modal qualifications (with requisite apologies to Dawkins), it becomes clear that we have no conception of what God's supreme perfection consists of. In other words, supreme perfection is something that exceeds human comprehension. Perhaps we could conceive of a Really, Really Good Being, a being that is as good as we could imagine. But such a conception would necessarily fall short of capturing God's goodness, for, again, God is the *best possible being*, not just the best we could imagine.

This, we think, is part of what it is to be God. God *must* be mysterious to us; His greatness *must* outstrip our powers of comprehension. He *must* be greater than created entities can even conceive or imagine. It should be noted that this commitment is very much in line with the popular belief among religious believers that God is a very, very special entity. God is so special, the usual line runs, that we cannot grasp Him or understand His essence. And so it seems that if God exists, then created beings must have no conception of Him or His perfection.

But here's the rub. *We do have a conception of God's perfection.* We say He is omnipotent, omniscient, omnibenevolent, and so on. We don't say his perfection entails, instead, looking good in a sundress, making the best martinis, telling the funniest jokes, or having a winning smile. So we in fact have a conception of His perfection after all. And yet if He existed, we wouldn't have a conception of His perfection; since we do, He doesn't. Thus God does not exist. That's the Ontological Argument *against* God's existence. What do you think?

We grant that our argument has its own odd (one might say *Presto!*) air to it. St. Anselm of Canterbury, the originator of the Ontological Argument, himself anticipated a version of our argument. Anselm claimed that arguments such as ours turn on two different senses of the term *conception*: one meaning "to have ideas about," and another "to have adequate ideas about." And so though we have ideas about God and His supreme perfection, we don't have *adequate* ideas about his perfection. Anselm may be right. But notice what his distinction does to the standard Ontological Argument. Once we say we don't have an *adequate* conception of God's supreme perfection, our confidence that such perfection entails existence should begin to wane. The only way to protect against our Ontological Argument *against* God's existence is to eviscerate the Ontological Argument for God's existence.

We have already said that we take the Ontological Argument to be a litmus test for a person's seriousness about God's existence. It is admittedly an argument that has the distinct whiff of error and trickery, but it is very difficult to spell out where it goes wrong. If one is already committed to the thought that there is no reasonable opposition to atheism, then the Ontological Argument will seem little more than a silly verbal trick, mere playacting at argument. But then criticism becomes all too easy, and as we've seen, all too facile. But we take the argument seriously, and we take religious belief seriously, too.

Sam Harris claims that "the honest criticism of religious faith [is] a moral and intellectual necessity" (2006: 57). We take it that he means that we are *obligated* to criticize religious faith, not that we couldn't help but do it. And he is surely correct. But honest criticism requires that we not construct straw men of religious believers and their arguments, and not treat clarifications and rebuttals with contempt. Instead, we must try to develop the best and most compelling versions of all the arguments. If we are to be reasonable and honest people who nevertheless disagree, we must be reasonable and honest in our disagreements.

VI. MORALITY AND THE NEW ATHEISM

The New Atheists frequently see their program as being tied closely to broader commitments regarding science. They see religion as necessarily opposed to the view of the world that science presents. Religion, they say, promotes a false and inferior vision of the world and human beings' place in it. Accordingly, the New Atheists not only believe that religious claims are false; they seek to rid the world of religious faith. For the New Atheists, it is not enough to see religious believers as demonstrably mistaken. On their view, religious believers *must be corrected*; they must be compelled to relinquish their false beliefs. On the New Atheist view, religious belief is like a gateway drug. Once one resolves to sit back while others believe irrational things, the game is over. Irrationality wins. And that would be a great tragedy for humanity. So religious belief must not only be refuted, it must be combated and defeated.

As we are atheists, we agree with much of this. The world would be better off, morally and intellectually, without religious belief. Indeed, we agree that most religious believers hold their beliefs in ways that are cognitively irresponsible. They believe on the basis of tradition, or habit, or someone else's say-so. They do not attend carefully enough to the arguments for and against their beliefs. And so on. But we part ways with the New Atheists when they assert that the case is closed with respect to the rationality or justification of religious belief. As we have been arguing in this chapter, the New Atheists systematically fail to consider the philosophically serious defenses of religion and religious belief. We hold that religious belief can be rationally defended, and that religious believers are not necessarily deluded or ignorant. Again, we hold that religious beliefs are false, not that religious believers are necessarily stupid. But once it is recognized that reasonable religious belief is possible, it is difficult to sustain the New Atheists' contempt for religious believers. It's hard to see religion as a plague that "poisons everything" and hastens the end of civilization.

We imagine that a New Atheist may respond as follows. He or she may say that the point is not to raise the argument over religious belief with philosophy professors, but with ordinary people. Whether philosophers can produce fancy arguments for religious belief is beside the point. The problem with religious belief, a New Atheist may say, is a problem with the religious beliefs of the man on the street, not in the Ivory Tower. The aim, they may continue, is not to instigate a philosophy seminar in which clever people trade arguments all day but to disabuse the common people of beliefs that are not only false, but dangerous to their own well-being and the well-being of others. Putting a distinctively New Atheist spin on this, he or she may conclude by claiming that the *religious worldview* is the enemy, and defeating it has little to do with philosophical arguments.

Fair enough. We take this line to be mistaken, but we'll take it up another time. For now, it helps us see why the New Atheists seem intent upon rejecting the totality of what religious believers hold. This means that the New Atheists are not content to show that there's no reason to believe in God or that common claims about angels, spirits, miracles, and so on are all bunk. The New Atheist takes aim at the religious believer's worldview, and that includes the religious believer's conception of morality.

We will take up questions regarding the connection between morality and religious belief in chapters 4 and 5. For now, it suffices to note that religious believers tend to hold that moral rules come from God, and that without God there could be no objective right and wrong, or good and bad. That is, the religious believer tends to hold that without God, there is no objective good and evil but only what someone or some group of people says is good and evil. Given that the New Atheists see as their target the worldview of the religious believer, they argue that the religious believer's *conception* of morality is defective. Put otherwise, if the religious worldview must go, and if the religious believer thinks that morality comes from God, then the religious believer's conception of morality must go as well.

We accept this. As we will argue in coming chapters, the view that God is necessary for there to be objective right and wrong is itself wrong. God plays no essential role in grounding objective morality. One can believe in objective, nonrelative morality and yet reject God's existence. God offers no help to moral theory.

But once we, along with the New Atheists, take this tack, we are left with showing how morality can be understood once belief in God is abandoned. Atheists must do moral philosophy. And here is where the New Atheists fall short.

When pressed on the origin of morality and the progressive moral development of Western civilization, Richard Dawkins simply dodges the question: "The onus is not on me to answer. For my purposes it is sufficient that they certainly have not come from religion" (2006: 270). His best hunch is that there is a changing moral "Zeitgeist," or Sprit of the Times, that moves and motivates people's ethical judgment. Further, he holds there is likely a native "kindness urge," one that inclines us to altruism in the same way that we have kinship urges that drive us to protect our own (2006: 221). He speculates that altruism and kindness were selected in our prehistory, partly because of the necessity of cooperation and partly as a display mechanism of health (and thereby a means for group status and procreative opportunities).

But this simply raises the question: What makes altruism *good*? What makes standing up for justice *right*? Evolutionary stories of how altruistic and kind acts benefit us perhaps explain why we have the beliefs that we ought to be altruistic and kind. But they do little to provide anything more than a biological just-so story as to the origin of the norms. They do nothing to explain why altruism is good.

Consider a few other New Atheists. Sam Harris offers a thoroughly deflated view of morality, holding that "saving a drowning child is no more of a moral duty than understanding a syllogism is a logical one" (2004: 172). The most Christopher Hitchens has to say about a positive source of morality is that "conscience is innate" (2007: 256), which amounts to not saying much. It is like explaining our capacity to do mathematics in terms of the innateness of our calculative abilities. And Michel Onfray, despite the fact that he takes nihilism (the belief in nothing, no moral law, no obligations at all) to be the product of religious belief, nevertheless seems to be a nihilist himself. He argues for a "post-Christian secularism," wherein there are no vestiges of Christian heritage in our moral vocabulary (2005: 56). He holds that only "atheistic atheism" (atheism that is without a God to oppose) is the only form of real morality. But Onfray never tells us what such a view looks like, only that we know it won't look like any monotheistic ethics. But is he serious? Will prohibitions against lying and murder be overcome? Would our inclinations to care for the sick be revealed to be unmotivated and perhaps immoral? No word, but only the promise that it will be "de-Christianized" (2005: 218), whatever that means. It is ironic that though Onfray criticizes many believers for their "nihilism" in reinterpreting Christian teachings to fit their moral inclinations, his own moral suggestions about morality are little more than naysaying.

The point here is crucial. In their effort to rid the world of what they take to be a dangerous and retrograde worldview, the New Atheists have thrown the baby out with the bathwater. They have affirmed that once belief in God is rejected, the world must become morally strange. They have conceded that without God, one can no longer believe that morality is a matter of objective rights and wrongs. They have asserted that without God, right actions are simply those that promote cooperation, or procreation, or stability amidst a population of creatures, and wrong acts are those that violate those objectives. To the religious believer, this seems an unacceptable proxy for morality; indeed, it seems to be a vision of the world that is *amoral*. Moreover, this amoralism confirms what religious believers tend to think of atheists, namely, that they are incapable of being moral because they are incapable of formulating a coherent morality.

In our view, this is a great philosophical and tactical error of the New Atheism. Again, we'll discuss nonreligious grounds for morality in the next chapter, so we will leave the philosophical correction of this line of thought for later. However, the tactical error is worth highlighting here. There is no need for the atheist to commit to a reductionist conception of morality, or to affirm that talking about good and evil is just a fancy way of talking about cooperation strategies. The atheist need not concede that once God is denied, the moral universe suddenly transforms. This is simply to accept the religious believer's claim to have a monopoly on commonsense morality; it is to allow the religious believer to claim that, in the end, atheists cannot really be moral. It is to cede the moral universe to religion.

VII. ACCOMMODATIONISM

Among the New Atheists, there is a term of abuse applied to those who treat religious belief and believers with even a shred of respect: *accommodationism.* In the eyes of the New Atheists, the accommodationist is someone who has lost his or her nerve, someone who, despite knowing what is right and true, colludes with the wrong and false. The accommodationist, the New Atheists say, finds it easier to just get along with all religious believers. The charge is that the accommodationist thereby abandons all the vigor, passion, and principle of real atheism, and thus betrays it. Moreover, it is alleged that in "playing nice" with religious believers, the accommodationist positively encourages religious belief. What's more, the accommodationist supposedly undoes the argumentative victories of the real atheist. In treating religious belief as reasonable, the accommodationist declines to subject religious belief to real criticism. In admitting that with complicated and difficult questions, there may be reasonable answers, the accommodationist purportedly soft-pedals the force of the critical points atheists propose.

There are a few things to make clear. First, we do not consider ourselves to be accommodationists. We think that the religious believer's core commitments are simply false; we also hold that adopting religious beliefs often has bad moral consequences. We stand, really, in firm opposition to religious belief and to the very idea of a supreme deity. As subsequent chapters will make clear, we are not just *atheists* (people who reject religious belief), but *antitheists* (people who think that religious belief is morally bad). In the coming chapters, we'll explain all of this more fully; for now, it is enough to say that we think there are compelling moral reasons to reject religious belief. In fact, we hold that the world would be a *morally worse* place if God existed.

Yet we know that the issues concerning God's existence and the justification of religious belief are frighteningly difficult. And we admit that we may be wrong about all of this. We of course don't think it's likely that we are wrong, but we acknowledge that in the past there have been many things about which we've been wrong and later discovered our error. We then changed our minds. Religious belief may yet be one of those things about which, given some new piece of evidence, a well-framed way of considering the standing evidence, or a novel argument, we should change our minds. We have intelligent and honest colleagues and friends who think we are dead wrong about God and religious belief. We argue with them all the time. We think they are wrong, but we do not thereby think they are stupid, ignorant, or evil on the basis of that fact. We simply hold ourselves open to correction from their side, as should any reasonable person in a dispute that is difficult and important. So far, there's nothing in our view that should count as accommodationism. We're simply committed to the responsible management of our cognitive lives.

We have not lost our nerve, nor have we said that atheists must always be nice to religious believers. In fact, in the coming chapters, we likely won't be nice by many peoples' standards. If you are a religious believer, we are going to say things that will bother and perhaps offend you. But we do so to instigate discussion, to highlight where we think the moral weight of the argument is on our side. We are confrontational so that discussion can continue, and so that it may be morally serious.

We expect that the New Atheists nonetheless will charge us with accommodationism because we wish to *continue* instead of *end* critical discussion with religious believers. Their attitude, it seems to us, is based in the confusion of belief evaluation with believer evaluation. We agree with the New Atheists that religious beliefs are false. But we also hold that one can be a religious believer and yet be cognitively aboveboard and reasonable. To repeat, whether someone is cognitively competent is a question of what one believes *given one's conception of the evidence*. One who is cognitively beyond the pale and incompetent is one who believes that the butler did it even though every piece of evidence one has strongly suggests that it was the maid.

Given that we live in a culture in which religious belief is the overwhelming norm, it is no wonder that so many people are religious believers; they are *raised* to believe as they do. When we add to this the relatively low level of exposure most people have to serious intellectual debate, it is no wonder that most people take themselves to be highly justified in holding their religious beliefs. To put the point more strongly, the average man on the street is justified in his religious beliefs in that his evidence and his reasons provide sufficient support for them. That he has a distorted sense of the evidence or an impoverished sense of what reasons can be raised against his views is irrelevant to the question of his general reasonableness. To be sure, the man on the street may be guilty of being gullible or cognitively careless or insufficiently curious, but whether he is justified in believing in God is a matter of what evidence he has. The proper response to him is not to dismiss him as an idiot, or belittle his beliefs as only so much superstition, but rather to compel him to consider a broader range of evidence and respond to forceful criticisms of his beliefs. This requires that we regard the man-on-the-street religious believer as reasonable and worth talking to as a fellow rational agent.

The New Atheists criticize our position as insufficiently firm. They may say that we are handing religious belief an easy victory in treating religious belief and believers as at least presumptively reasonable and worthy of extended argument. Yet in our view, it is positively strange that the Enlightenment tradition, one committed to the openness of inquiry and the freedom of debate, could yield a form of rationalism that is in principle closed to treating its opposition with intellectual regard. It is a form of dogmatism we find both vicious and counterproductive. If the aim is to rid the world of superstition and irrational beliefs, those who hold such beliefs must be *argued* out of them. The desired result cannot be achieved by New Atheist browbeating and bluster. We must argue. And until we're ready to acknowledge that religious believers can be reasonable, no real argument can commence.

CHAPTER FOUR

ETHICS WITHOUT GOD

✣

Our discussion thus far has been mostly preliminary. We have made the case for thinking that argumentative engagement among religious believers and atheists is desirable; in fact, we have argued for the stronger thesis that such engagement is required by the mandates of cognitive responsibility. Along the way, we have repeatedly claimed that, on a clear view of the matter, atheism is a position that religious believers must regard as reasonable. Our main reason for this claim so far has been that atheism is driven by an ethics of belief that prizes reason, argument, and evidence. Atheists are reasonable, then, insofar as they can offer reasons for their position; they can provide criticisms of religious belief and offer positive arguments for their own beliefs.

But now we want to argue that atheists can be reasonable in a deeper sense. To be specific, we seek in this chapter to correct some of the more prominent misconceptions religious believers have of the *moral* commitments that follow from atheism. As we have mentioned, religious believers typically contend that atheism is equivalent to immoralism or nihilism. They see atheism as simple naysaying skepticism that makes no positive proposal for how one ought to live. Some contend that atheism is a radical form of relativism, the view that good and evil are simply a matter of someone's say-so or some culture's norms. In any case, they see atheists as unable to recognize real and objective goods and evils.

✓ false

Accordingly, they tend to hold that atheists are immoral, antagonistic, untrustworthy, and unable to behave responsibly.

As is clear by now, we reject this common image of the atheist. We hold that the difference between moral and immoral people is a difference of behavior and character; religious belief or lack thereof is irrelevant. Moreover, atheism is capable of supporting all commitments regarding morality that religious believers often see as requiring religious belief. Consequently, atheists are not properly depicted as morally alien to religious believers. There is nothing in the intellectual commitments of atheism that requires immoralism, relativism, or nihilism; thus, there is no reason for religious believers to look upon atheists as morally suspect. As far as morality is concerned, atheists and religious believers can have much in common. In this chapter, we shall present our case for this view.

Here's how we will proceed. First, we will examine the claim that morality depends on God. We will argue that this view, though popular, is highly contestable and in fact raises serious problems for the religious believer. Then, we will canvass many compelling conceptions of morality that are decidedly nonreligious. The aim of the chapter, then, is to show the reader that the common view about the relation of morality to religious belief is far less simple than often thought and that atheists can adopt the view that there are objective rights and wrongs, and goods and evils.

I. ATHEISM AND IMMORALISM

Atheists are unpopular. They are perceived as arrogant, selfish, mean-spirited, close-minded, opportunistic, and untrustworthy. But why? The answer regularly given is that without a belief in God, an afterlife, or heaven and hell, one has no reason to be moral; since the atheist denies everything upon which morality rests, he or she has no morality at all.

Dostoevsky's angry atheist in the *Brothers Karamazov*, Rakitin, is usually invoked to capture the atheist perspective on morality. Rakitin says, "without God and immortal life? All things are lawful . . . a clever man can do what he likes." Crucially, according to Rakitin, both God and immortal life are required—we need both a perfect legislator and an infallible system of retribution and reward to be motivated to follow moral rules. According to Rakitin, without the threat of eternal punishment for immorality, there wouldn't be any reason to refrain from stealing, cheating, lying, murdering, raping, and so on. In fact, political commentator and Christian apologist Dinesh D'Souza concludes that this libertine opportunity is the "perennial appeal of atheism":

> [I]t gets rid of the stern fellow with the long beard and liberates us for the pleasures of sin and depravity. The atheist seeks to get rid of moral judgment by getting rid of the judge. (2007: 272)

Because there is "no hell to pay for violating the commandment(s)," (2007: 270) atheism is, by D'Souza's lights, a positive revolt against morality.

We think that D'Souza has articulated a very popular thought about atheists. However, there are at least two confusions in D'Souza's remark. First, he mistakes atheist criticisms of particular rules of conduct for an endorsement of immoralism. Atheists indeed criticize many principles of conduct that are popular among religious believers. The atheist's view is not that all principles of conduct are to be dismissed, but rather that religious believers often adopt principles of conduct that are *morally objectionable.* Consider those religious believers who take their moral instruction from the Bible. We can find many moral rules in the stories and injunctions in the Old and New Testaments that we have powerful *moral* reasons to reject. For example, Paul enjoined that men not suffer a woman teaching (I Timothy 2:11–14), Moses insisted that we execute anyone we even suspect is a witch (Exodus 22:18), and Jesus taught that divorce is unlawful (Mark 10:1–12) except in cases of infidelity (Matthew 5:31). This last principle is especially troublesome since it means that domestic abuse, no matter how violent and injurious, is an insufficient ground for dissolving a marriage.

What D'Souza overlooks is that the atheist's rejection of these biblical injunctions is driven by the judgment that they are *morally wrong*. The only reason one would adopt them is that one takes God's word to be definitive when it comes to moral issues. But there certainly are compelling—and we think conclusive—moral reasons *not* to follow those rules. It doesn't make one an immoralist to insist that we should do away with rules that say, with Paul, that women cannot have any authority; or, with Moses, that all suspected witches must die; or, with Jesus, that wives may not leave husbands who beat them. Quite the contrary! Rejecting these biblical prescriptions is *required* by morality. In rejecting these rules of human conduct, the atheist is most certainly not advocating immoralism, nor is the rejection part of an attempt to escape from morality. The atheist is advocating a *better morality*.

Second, D'Souza confuses self-interested motives with properly moral motives. D'Souza, along with many other religious believers, seems to think that without the threat of eternal punishment for breaking commandments, the atheist has no reason to be good. But, we ask, is *this* the overriding reason why religious believers are good? Are they good simply because they want to avoid eternal hellfire? D'Souza's view entails that religious believers would be moral criminals—stealing, lying, cheating, murdering, raping, torturing monsters—were it not for God's watchful eye and credible threat of eternal damnation. D'Souza holds, in other words, that religious believers are good because they believe that being good *pays*.

this.

But being good simply to win a reward or avoid a punishment is not really being *good*, is it? It is simply being *prudent*, simply acting in one's best interest, and simply looking out for oneself. Such are the motives of laboratory rats, not moral agents. That is, there is a distinction between self-interest and morality. The self-interested agent performs those acts that he or she reckons will further his or her interests. The moral agent, by contrast, performs those acts that he or she reckons are right; accordingly, in deliberating about what to do, the moral agent consults reasons *other than* those concerning his or her own interests. Put otherwise, the good person behaves morally *because that is the right thing to do*. The test for really being *good*, then, is how one behaves when one knows one could do wrong without being caught. → *character*

One thing to note is that religious believers of D'Souza's kind never allow themselves to be put to this test. They hold that God is always watching, and so there is never the possibility of doing wrong without being caught. Because they hold that only the threat of punishment can motivate moral behavior, it is hard to see how D'Souza's religious believers can see *themselves* as ever really being good. If you think you're always being watched by someone who will punish you for your misdeeds, and if the avoidance of that punishment is your overriding motive, then you never do good for its own sake; you never do the right thing *because* it is right. Atheists, by contrast, don't believe in a God who is watching their every move. Consequently, atheists are regularly testing their own goodness; when they do the right thing, they do so because they have consulted their moral reasons.

If you accept the distinction between self-interest and morality, then you must see that it is D'Souza who is the immoralist. Once his view is unpacked, we find that D'Souza holds that *no one ever acts morally*; at best, individuals act in accordance with moral rules for self-interested reasons. But to do the right thing for reasons of self-interest is not *really*

99

to do the right thing. It's to do the advantageous thing, which in some cases happens to coincide with the right thing. If, on the other hand, you believe that it is possible for people to act morally, then you must admit that the avoidance of punishment is not the only consideration that could motivate action. And this, in turn, means that atheists can be moral agents, and D'Souza's argument collapses. Our suggestion, of course, is that we should abandon the idea that only the threat of punishment can motivate good behavior; we believe, against D'Souza, that it is possible to be good for its own sake. We suspect that many religious believers will agree with us.

These confusions aside, there is another questionable commitment underlying D'Souza's comment. D'Souza supposes that there can be no morality at all without God. Again, it is commonly thought that God is necessary not only to provide people with sufficient motivation to be good, but for there to be a difference between good and evil at all. In short, D'Souza thinks that either there's a God to mandate what is good and what is evil, or nothing is good or evil at all. Since it says that God is necessary to found morality, let's call this proposal *the foundational claim*. Laura Schlessinger and Stewart Vogel pose it dramatically in their recent book on the Ten Commandments:

> If the values are not God-derived, they come from fads and favorites ...laziness...selfishness...and a personal desire to get away with anything under the protection of nonjudgmentalism.... (1998: 4)

Conservative political critic Ann Coulter says essentially the same thing:

> Without this fundamental understanding of man's place in the world, we risk being lured into misguided pursuits, including bestiality, slavery, and PETA membership. (2007: 3)

biblical commentator J. I. Packer agrees:

> The world becomes a strange, mad, painful place, and a life in it disappointing and unpleasant business, for those who do not know about God. Disregard the study of God, and you sentence yourself to stumble and blunder through it blindfolded, as it were, with no sense of direction and no understanding of what surrounds you. (1973: 19)

As these quotations indicate, the foundational claim holds that either ethical values are founded by God and hence are objective and binding, or values are knit from the cloth of fleeting interest and hence are merely subjective and certainly not binding for anyone who wishes to renounce them. God is the necessary foundation for morality; without Him, there is no morality, only preference and power. Again, this is a highly popular view. In the following sections, however, we will show how the foundational claim goes awry. We will show that God's commanding something does not guarantee that what is commanded is objectively morally correct. In the sixth section of this chapter— *Goodness without God*—we will outline a handful of the going theories of how there can be objective and binding moral rules without God.

II. GOD AND MORALITY

The claim that we need God's authority for there to be objective right and wrong is understandable. Ethical decisions are often difficult, sometimes even heart-wrenching. There are cases in which we are unsure of what is valuable or how values of different kinds can be compared. For example, part of what makes moral questions concerning the environment so difficult is that they often ask us to consider the moral entitlements of creatures that are not themselves moral agents, as well as members of future generations who do not yet exist. It is hard to decide how much of a moral claim rain forests or future people have in our current deliberations about global warming. But moral dilemmas can be difficult even when the values at stake are pretty clear. We can all agree that life is valuable, suffering is bad, and people should be allowed to live their lives as they see fit (within certain obvious constraints). These ideas are clear enough for most people. Problems arise when these widely recognized ethical principles conflict with one another. Consider two obvious examples. Abortion pits the rights of pregnant women to determine the use of their bodies against the value of nascent human life. Dilemmas about euthanasia arise from the conflict between preventing further suffering and one choosing how one's life ends on one side and the intrinsic value of life on the other.

Nobody denies the moral seriousness of such issues, and given that humans are fallible and few of our solutions are acceptable to all, it is often the case that when confronted with a serious moral dilemma, people feel perplexed to the point of paralysis. Having God's view on the matter, it is regularly thought, would be very helpful. Although we may not be smart enough to answer the heavy questions ourselves, God is smart enough not only to have the answers but also to have written them down for us (or at least have had someone write it down for Him). Appeal to God's take on these matters is a clear and attractive option when things are so conflicted and difficult for us. God serves, as D'Souza says, as the Judge, the one who has the Last Word about morality.

It is important to distinguish two distinct ways of cashing out the thought that God resolves ethical dilemmas for us. On one hand is the view that God provides us with *guidance*. God is all-knowing, and therefore his say-so is a reliable guide to the truth about some ethical issue.

On the other hand is the view that God is the *ground* for morality: God is all-powerful, and therefore his say-so makes it so; that is, God's commands and judgments are the source and ground for ethical truths. On the first view, God is the supreme moral expert who gives unfailingly moral, reliable counsel. On the second view, God is the supreme moral architect who creates right and wrong by commanding and forbidding actions.

To be sure, the first view is regularly taken to be a consequence of the second view. God is a moral expert who provides unfailingly reliable moral guidance *because* the entire structure of morality is the product of His will. In other words, God's commanding us to do something—say, honor our parents—not only makes it so we have the obligation to honor our parents; we learn that we are supposed to honor our parents. God's commands both *create* obligations and *inform* us what those obligations are.

Atheists are often pressed by religious believers on the question of how there could be morality without God. We see now that this question can be parsed into two separate questions:

1. Without God's *guidance*, how do you know that you have the right answers to ethical questions?
2. Without God's *grounding*, how are there any right answers to ethical questions?

Recall Schlessinger's version of the foundational claim. She says that either God makes the rules (and so they are objective and binding) or we do (and so they are subjective and nonbinding). Divine grounding is, Schlessinger claims, the only morally acceptable option, and as a consequence, we must take God's commands as offering moral guidance.

III. EUTHYPHRO'S PROBLEM

It is important to note that the question of the nature and ground of morality is very old. It was a pressing question in antiquity, and classical Athens was a place where many struggled with it. Plato wrestled seriously with the issue, and he posed the first and still most serious challenge to the divine grounding thesis in one of his early dialogues, *Euthyphro*. In the dialogue, Socrates, Plato's mentor and a regular character in his dialogues, asked a local holy man, Euthyphro, to define *piety*. After a few attempts to answer Socrates' question, Euthyphro enunciated a version of the divine grounding theory:

> I would certainly say that the pious is what all the gods love, and the opposite, what all the gods hate, is the impious. (*Euthyphro* 9e)

Euthyphro's definition is complicated because he was a polytheist. This means that he held that there are lots of gods: some are gods of love (Aphrodite), war (Ares), the underworld (Hades), and so on. These gods disagree about a number of things, but when they agree on something, it is important. Euthyphro thought that when all these gods agree that something is good, it must be good. This seems reasonable as far as it goes, since we ourselves take our best answers to be the ones around which reasonable people can find agreement. But Socrates posed an important challenge to Euthyphro's view. Socrates asked:

> Is the pious loved by the gods because it is pious, or is it pious because the gods love it? (*Euthyphro* 10a)

Let us explain that a bit. Socrates presented Euthyphro with what logicians call a *dilemma*, an either-or statement presenting two options, from which Euthyphro must choose exactly one. Euthyphro must say either that the pious things are loved by the gods because they are pious, or he must say that pious things are pious because the gods love them. But either option does damage to the claim that morality must be divinely grounded. Here's why. Let's take for example acts of charity. If, on the one hand, the gods love acts of charity *because* such acts are pious, then the gods are not the ground for piety. The piety of acts of charity consists of something about the nature of those acts, and it is this nature that the gods see and approve of. But, importantly, their commands don't make acts of charity good; rather, the gods command acts of charity *because* they see that such acts are good. So if pious acts are loved by the gods because they are pious acts, the gods are at best reliable moral experts and not moral architects; they offer expert advice about how to behave, but they do not provide the ground for morality.

But God was supposed to provide the ground for morality! So let's consider the other option open to Euthyphro. If, on the other hand, acts of charity are pious simply in virtue of the fact that the gods approve of them, then the gods surely do ground morality. But this view comes at a price. We ask: Why are acts of charity morally preferable to, say, building a really big fire or playing countless rounds of computer solitaire? If the moral goodness of acts of charity comes simply from the gods' approval of such acts, then we cannot point to any moral feature of charity itself that makes it worthy of the approval of the gods. Moreover, if acts of charity are pious entirely because the gods like them, then we can't say *why* they like them. This puts us in very strange moral territory. Good and evil (or piety and impiety) are, on the view we're considering, a matter of the gods' whim. What, after all, makes charity morally special? And if we can say what makes charity so special, then we've denied that the gods' commands ground morality. We are left simply with saying that the gods make the rules. There's no way to say that those rules are morally correct or even appropriate.

Hence Euthyphro's problem: It is either the case that in approving of acts of charity, the gods are responding to some fact about charity that makes it worthy of moral approval, or it is the case that in approving of acts of charity, the gods are not responding to any fact about acts of that kind but are simply expressing a preference for charity. The first option concedes that the moral quality that makes acts of charity worthy of the gods' approval is independent of the gods and rejects the thesis that morality depends on the gods. The second option indeed makes morality depend on the gods, but it requires one to say that morality is simply a matter of the gods' whim; there is no reason the gods happen to approve of acts of charity or disapprove of acts of murder. The first option denies that morality depends on the gods because it recognizes moral properties that are independent of the gods; the second option makes morality simply a matter of the whim of the gods. Neither option seems promising for the thesis that morality depends upon God.

Modern-day religious believers who seek to ground morality in God tend to be monotheistic. They might claim that Euthyphro's Problem arises only for polytheists. They might say that Euthyphro must confront the problem Socrates raised because he was trying to split the difference between the gods of war, love, and death. We imagine them continuing that given the brood of gods Euthyphro recognizes, it's no wonder Euthyphro couldn't find a divine grounding for morality. His gods operated according to wildly different moral rules! That is, religious believers will argue that once one accepts monotheism, Euthyphro's Problem dissolves.

But this response does not succeed. The problem Socrates posed to Euthyphro isn't a problem for the polytheist alone. Euthyphro's Problem presents the monotheist with a similarly crushing dilemma. To see this, take the prohibition against murder in the Ten Commandments. We pose Socrates' dilemma: Does God prohibit murder because murder is wrong, or is murder wrong because God prohibits it? If you think that

God prohibits murder because it is wrong, then in commanding us to not murder, God is at best offering guidance about the wrongness of murder (but don't we already know murder is wrong, since murder is unjustified killing?); he is not thereby making murder wrong in saying that it is. The fact that He commands us to not murder is irrelevant to the wrongness of murder. For if God commands against murder *because* murder is wrong, then its wrongness is not the product of His prohibition; it is the explanation of the prohibition. Thus morality is independent of God; God does not ground morality.

But the remaining option in the dilemma is also unwelcome. Say that murder is wrong simply because God commands us to not murder. Murder is wrong *because* God says so. We ask: *why* does God say murder is wrong? Now it seems to us that the moral wrongness of murder is in the murdering, the killing of another for no morally justifying reason. Life's value, it seems, is something you can't miss, and no measure of commands, threats, or entreaties could correct someone who happens to not get it. And so the unjustified ending of a life seems an obvious wrong, because life is valuable. God's commands don't make murder wrong—it just is wrong, and its wrongness is explained by the fact that life is a valuable thing. But if, as the second option in the dilemma insists, God's say-so really does make murder wrong, then before God prohibited murder, there was no such thing as wrongly killing another person.

This seems to turn the moral world entirely upside down! On the divine grounding theory, the rule that we mustn't kill others is correct not because their lives are valuable but because God commands us not to murder. By extension, this view has it that we needn't give to charities because we should reduce suffering but simply because God says we should. We should take care of our children and foster their development not because their well-being is valuable and we are responsible for our children, but rather because God says we should.

The point is that if you accept the second option in the dilemma presented by Socrates, you must hold that God's commands are the sole source of moral goodness. The good is simply the God-commanded. This renders empty all moral nuance and richness of actually living a good life. Moreover, it renders all moral inquiry and deliberation irrelevant, if not positively dangerous. In this view, moral responsibility and living a good life do not call for careful moral contemplation and reflection. Living well simply requires that you follow orders. Being good is easy after all.

Adopting the second option in Socrates' dilemma leaves one with an impoverished conception of the moral life. We, the authors, think this is a heavy price to pay, and it should be a sufficient reason for abandoning the view that good things are good because God commands them. But maybe the cost of upholding this view is acceptable to you. So let's raise a few additional difficulties.

IV. GOD AND MORAL OBJECTIVITY

If God's say-so makes good acts good and bad acts bad, then it is hard to see how His claims are objective in the way we normally think about objectivity. In the more general cases, a claim is objectively true when its truth does not depend on whether anybody believes it, recognizes it, accepts it, or holds it true. That Saturn has rings is true independently of whether we believe it. That lead atoms are heavier than hydrogen atoms is true whether anybody ever thought about it. A claim is subjectively true, on the other hand, when it is made true by someone holding it true. And so chocolate is tastier than vanilla for those who hold it is. The average knock-knock joke is funnier than David Letterman's best monologue, for those who have that preference. In these cases, *having the pref-*

erence for X over Y makes it true that *X is better than Y*, for in these contexts *X is better than Y* simply means *I prefer X to Y*.

Now, as we saw above, those who hold that God is necessary for morality claim to be concerned with the objectivity of morality. They contend that without God, morality collapses into merely subjective preferences. But we now see that the view that murder is wrong because God forbids it has the following ironic implication: the truths of morality depend on God's say-so. And so, at least by normal standards regarding the meanings of the terms *objective* and *subjective*, if "murder is wrong" is true due to the fact that God commands us not to murder, then it is a *subjective* truth that murder is wrong. That is to say, on the view under consideration, *murder is wrong* is true in the same way that *chocolate is tastier than vanilla* is true. Instead of being a way of establishing the *objectivity* of moral truths, the view that God grounds morality actually entails that morality is relative to God's perspective.

Granted, we're talking about *God's* perspective here. But once one adopts the second option in the Socrates' question, one must assert that there's nothing about the nature of, say, murder that gives God a moral reason to prohibit it. Recall the first option conceded that God commands us not to murder due to the fact that murder is wrong; it is for this reason that the first option fails to sustain the thesis that God is the ground of morality. So once one rejects the first option, one must assert that God prohibits murder *for no moral reason*. He prohibits murder, and favors honoring one's parents, for roughly the same reason you like chocolate ice cream; namely, it appeals to you. You do not favor chocolate ice cream for any reason other than that it tastes good to you. Importantly, your preference for chocolate is not the result of any special knowledge you have about ice cream, and it is not the result of some special study you've undertaken. Your preference for chocolate ice cream is something you simply find yourself with. And knowing, for example, that chocolate ice cream is worse for your health than strawberry does not change the way chocolate tastes to you relative to strawberry; you still prefer the taste of chocolate (though now you may order strawberry more often).

In short, the view that says that murder is wrong because God forbids it requires one to say that God's commandments are not the product of God's moral reasons or even of God's moral knowledge because, on this view, there are no moral reasons and there is no moral knowledge. In forbidding murder and requiring us to honor our parents, God is not responding to moral facts about the badness of murder or the goodness of honoring one's parents. On this view, for God, there are no moral facts until He creates them by issuing commandments. Consequently, when God commands us to not murder, He is acting according to His whim.

And once one adopts this view, we simply ask: Why is God's perspective any better than yours (or ours)? If the truths are subjective—if, to return to our example, there's nothing about murder that makes it worth forbidding—then nobody is in any better position to judge than any other. In fact, there's no judging at all but only preferring. That's what subjective truths are. And unless one can explain *why* God forbids murder, then one cannot explain why His perspective is any better than any other. But if there is a reason why God forbids murder, then God's commands are the products of His assessment of the moral reasons concerning murder, and morality does not require God for its grounding after all. So we reach a surprising conclusion: If morality depends on God, then all morality is subjective. The lesson is, then, the only way to make morality objective is to make it independent of God's commands.

Before moving on, we should mention briefly a likely response to the foregoing argument. A religious believer may say that God is indeed the ground for morality, and embrace fully the second option in Socrates' question: murder is wrong simply because God forbids it. In response to our question about why God's perspective matters, the religious believer may say one of the following: God's perspective matters because God is special or because it's *God's* perspective. But neither reply is very promising. The *God is special* response, encountered earlier in our discussion of *Presto!* arguments, simply pushes the question back: How can God be special if there's nothing about acts of murder that provides God with reasons to forbid them? The second response, which holds that God's perspective matters simply in virtue of its being God's is puzzling. We suspect that this reply is driven by the D'Souza intuition that God has the power to dole out eternal punishment. God's the boss, so what He says matters. But this reply flies directly into the teeth of our argument regarding the distinction between self-interest and morality. That is, the reply concedes that the force of God's commands derives simply from His power. We should do what He commands because it *pays*. In which case, God's commands have no *moral* force at all.

V. MORAL INTERPRETATION AND MORAL REASONING

Let's move now to a second problem with the thought that God is the ground of morality. The trouble with God's commandments is that they're like ordinary rules and regulations in that we must often use our own autonomous judgment to interpret, implement, and understand them. It is often surprisingly difficult to interpret what moral lessons God is trying to get across. The Ten Commandments and the Golden Rule are good places to start for moral instruction. But even with these, it is unclear how to take those rules as really determining the best moral course for our actions. (At this point, we direct our reader to appendix B.)

Take, for example, the Golden Rule. As we all know, it says, "Do unto others as you would have them do unto you." This sounds like good advice. But what guidance does it really offer? What does it mean? Seriously.

Our view is that the Golden Rule is actually not of any use unless we already have a good and independent idea of what morality requires of us. Let us consider a simple example. A father faces a situation in which he must enforce his children's 7 PM bedtime. How does the Golden Rule bear on this? Suppose that the father himself wants to stay up late—way beyond 7 PM—and read. Does that mean he should let his children stay up late, too? If he enforces the bedtime, does it mean that *he* should go to bed at 7 PM as well? What does the Golden Rule recommend in this case? Or let's change the situation a little bit. The father determines that the kids should go to bed at 7 PM and he gets to stay up, but now the kids keep sneaking out of their rooms, quietly engaging in activities other than sleep. How does the Golden Rule help here? If the father himself wishes his own parents had been stricter and punished him more seriously even for minor infractions, then may he beat his children for their misdeeds? Alternately, if the father doesn't like people telling him what to do and certainly doesn't like being punished, then may he simply ignore the various rustlings in the kitchen, tappings on the computer, and giggles from the stairwell for all hours of the night? What course of action would count as satisfying the *do unto others as you would have them do unto you* rule? Given the way the rule is stated, it's not clear what God's moral advice is.

The father-and-bedtime-enforcement scenario is, as we said, simple. Some may find it silly. But it shows something important. Without a properly functioning independent moral system already in place, the Golden Rule is either entirely empty of content or utterly relativist in its application. We say it is empty of content because it seems that whoever uses the rule must provide the content. And it is relativist because it holds that the correctness of an action depends entirely on how the person acting would like to be treated. To see this, consider another example. We have a friend who is an oncologist who regularly asserts that, should she develop an inoperative and terminal form of cancer, she'd rather have her physician lie to her than be told the truth about her condition. Does the Golden Rule advise her to lie to her own patients when they test positive for inoperative and terminal cancer? There's a sense in which, by doing so, she would be treating others as she'd like to be treated. But note that if she happened to have another set of preferences concerning how she'd like to be treated in the given case, a different act would be morally required by the Golden Rule. Not an especially effective recipe for absolute and objective morality, is it?

Some will no doubt charge us with misinterpreting the Golden Rule. They will say that the Rule calls us to treat others how they would want us to treat them. Let's leave aside for now the issue about how we can know when an interpretation of a purported moral rule is mistaken, and just consider the revision. It still seems to us horribly relativistic. Let's say you catch a burglar on the street just as she's making her getaway from a house she robbed. Now she'd *like* for you to simply let her go. Letting her go would be treating her as she'd like you to treat her. But letting her go would be obviously wrong. Perhaps the wrongness has to do with the fact that a third party—namely, the person who owns the house that was robbed—is involved. Letting the thief go would be to treat the homeowner in a way that he would not like to be treated; he'd rather you hold the thief and call the police. So someone will have to be treated in a way that runs against the Golden Rule. Who shall it be? The Golden Rule offers no advice. To determine that we should hold the thief and call the police, we need recourse to another moral rule and perhaps in addition a rule that tells us how to prioritize other moral rules.

There's a lot more to say about these cases. The upshot thus far is that unless we humans already have good moral judgment, we cannot make any good sense of God's attempts to guide us. Put otherwise, the moral instruction God gives us must piggyback on the good moral sense we already have. To be moral, we must exercise our own moral judgment. And this requires more of us than simply following God's rules. Moral life requires us to reason morally, to think moral thoughts not contained in God's commands, and to go beyond God's rules.

The need for independent moral reasoning is in high relief when God's instructions may be plausibly interpreted to run counter to good moral sense. Here is an example. Samuel was one of the judges in Israel, and he instructed Saul, the king, on how to handle a tribe living in the Promised Land who resisted Israel's expansion:

> Go now upon the Amelekites and destroy them, and put their property under ban. Spare no one: put them all to death, men and women, children and babes in arms, herds and flocks, camels and asses. (I Samuel 15:3)

So Saul went out and "cut the Amelekites to pieces," he "destroyed all the people, putting them all to the sword" (15:7–8). But he didn't kill all the cattle and lambs. He kept the choice ones to sacrifice later. When Samuel and God found out that Saul had spared these animals, they were angry. Samuel chastised Saul: "Obedience is better than sacrifice" (15:22). And then Samuel relieved Saul of his position as king.

So what is the lesson of this story? It is hard to tell, really. Samuel asserts that obedience is better than sacrifice. But that can't be the moral point of the story. We could extend Samuel's thought and say that it might be that obedience to God is the most important thing, and even if you try to do better (kill *almost* everyone and make sacrifices of the rest), you're in for trouble. On this reading, it certainly seems that following God's orders is more important than all the lives of those

Amelekite men, women, children, and babes in arms. Furthermore, it's a plausible moral that Saul, after having hacked children and babies to pieces with a sword but saving the cows, was morally wrong *for not killing the cows*.

This, again, is the morally upside-down universe that one must inhabit if one thinks that God's commands are the only morally significant data available to moral agents. Nobody in their right mind, at least nowadays, would think that the lesson is that it would have been morally preferable for Saul to kill every member of an opposing religion and destroy their property, including their animals. And since we know that *that* can't be God's moral lesson, we know to look elsewhere. Perhaps the lesson of Samuel and Saul is just that Saul was too proud and thought he could put a cherry on top of doing his duty—he was a show-off. Or perhaps it is a lesson about how Samuel could have been clearer about what was expected—good managers anticipate where mistakes can be made.

But we know that God's lesson just can't be *kill 'em all*. Why? Because we know that would be wrong. For us to come up with even plausible interpretations of biblical passages that purport to teach us about morality, we have to already be good at thinking about what is right and wrong. In fact, for us to even judge whether an interpretation of a biblical lesson is good or bad we must exercise some fairly sophisticated moral thought. To interpret God's guidance in scripture at all responsibly, we must already be fairly good at solving moral problems, thinking critically about moral questions, and recognizing good and evil for what they are.

We do this all the time. Consider that Paul clearly endorsed slavery, enjoining all slaves to "obey your earthly masters . . . as slaves of Christ" (Ephesians 6:5-6). Jesus held that one cannot follow him properly unless one *hates* (in Greek, the word is the unambiguous *miseo*) one's father, mother, sisters, brothers, wife, children, even one's own life (Luke 14:26).

But when we confront biblical passages that seem obviously beyond the pale when interpreted literally, we conclude that they must be interpreted metaphorically, or we say that there were extenuating circumstances that explain the passage, or we go to great lengths to find linguistic loopholes to ensure that God does not give that kind of advice. The point is that even if one holds that we need God's guidance in dealing with moral questions, one must also hold that we are capable of being good without His guidance. Otherwise, ironically, we couldn't make use of His help.

The question with which we began is how one could be good without God. The answer is perhaps surprising. We, atheist and religious believer alike, are good independently of God all the time. And even in the religious believer's own view, we *must* exercise our independent moral judgment if we are to make proper sense of God's moral instructions. It seems, then, that atheists and religious believers are in agreement on at least one highly significant issue: living well, being good, and doing the right thing are not achievable by simply following orders, even if the orders are thought to come from God. To be good, one must exercise one's own moral judgment. In other words, one can be good without God.

Many Christians have recognized this point. Paul himself notes that the "Gentiles," those who have not received God's laws, nevertheless "carry out its percepts by the light of nature" (Romans 2:14). That is, Paul recognized that humans *can* be moral without God's explicit guidance because they partake in and are expressions of the Natural Law. Consequently, "they are their own law, for they display the effects of the law inscribed in their hearts," (2:15) and they do this by arguing and thinking through the various sides of difficult issues. Ultimately, "their conscience is called as their witness" (Romans 2:15). Even the Romans and Greeks (who worship the licentious Olympians), the Persians (who worship Ahura Mazda), and the Egyptians (who worship their various animal-headed gods) nevertheless protect property, establish fair exchange, prohibit murder and lying, and so on. They do this as expressions of their *conscience*. St. Thomas Aquinas glossed Paul in his *Summa Theologica* and noted clearly that it is the function of humans as rational creatures that makes them capable of partaking in the "eternal reason" that undergirds moral truths. According to Aquinas, humans naturally apprehend the Natural Law (*Treatise on Law*, Questions 90–97).

It is important to note that this *Natural Law* tradition in religious ethics concedes everything we have said thus far about the supposed dependence of morality upon God. According to the Natural Law tradition, God is not the exclusive source of ethical insight; independent human reason can arrive reliably at moral truths. It is conceded that the heathen Romans and Greeks were capable of being good without God. In fact, on the Natural Law view, Ancient Greeks and Romans were capable of goodness despite the fact that they worshipped false gods. What makes all the difference on this Natural Law view is that people arrive at their considered moral views with their reason directing them and with the freedom of their own conscience. In the Natural Law tradition, humans are capable of morality only when they are allowed intellectual freedom. Again, to be good, one must exercise one's powers of moral reason. No one is good in virtue of rote obedience to commands, even if those commands come from God.

Importantly, atheists stand squarely with the Natural Law theorists here. In fact, in the next chapter, we will show that many adopt atheism precisely *because* they recognize the value of reason and freedom of conscience. However, before we present our moral case for atheism, we must show that there are compelling theories about the nature of morality that make no appeal at all to God.

VI. GOODNESS WITHOUT GOD:
FOUR THEORIES

A question may still be lingering for many readers: If God isn't the source of objective morality, then who or what is? The short answer is that we don't know. The ultimate source or ground of objective morality is the subject of an exciting philosophical debate that has been going strong for thousands of years, at least since the time of the Ancient Greeks (that's roughly the fifth century BCE). Although it's not clear which view is correct, it is clear that there are many powerful contenders. Accordingly, the question of the ultimate ground for morality is one about which there is room for reasonable disagreement. We, the authors, are professional philosophers, and we have our own positions on the matter at hand. Importantly, we—again, the authors—disagree with each other over the basis of morality. It is a subject of ongoing philosophical debate between us. Though we disagree over the philosophical question about the grounding for morality, we nonetheless see each other as reasonable. We each see the other as *wrong* about morality's ground, but that does not preclude either of.us from seeing the other as careful, sincere, honest, and well informed. So it makes sense for us to regularly take up the debate together.

In the following section, we want to present sketches of a few theories as to how there can be nondivine sources of right and wrong. They do not fit together into a coherent story. In fact, the ongoing debates between the various options are quite raucous. Our discussion here will not present the views in their full detail; our objective is only to present pieces of them to show that it is possible to think about ethics without having to think about God. We will introduce the central thoughts behind each program as what we see as the clearest and most plausible answers to simple ethical questions.

To begin: Why shouldn't people kick puppies? We mean *really* kick them, with full force and for no reason. It seems wrong to do that. But what makes it wrong? An obvious thought is that one shouldn't kick puppies because kicking them hurts them. Pain is a bad thing. All people know that, especially about their own pain. But once it's clear that others have relevantly similar pains when injured, we make a moral discovery: pain is bad, no matter who experiences it. And the same goes for pleasure. We serve our friends tall glasses of icy lemonade on hot days because lemonade is wonderful when you're hot and thirsty. Pleasures are good, and they are good no matter who experiences them. Consequently, as pleasures are good and pains are bad, we have a perfectly natural moral system taking shape wherein we should promote pleasure and decrease pain. *Hedonism* (from the Greek *hedone*, which means "pleasure") is the name for such a view. It was widely held in classical Rome by the Epicureans, and it was revived in eighteenth-century England by the Utilitarians.

Now, it should be noted that *hedonism* is popularly used as a term of moral disapproval. To call someone a hedonist is to call that person a selfish and shortsighted slave to temporary titillations. One pictures a drunk Roman, reclining on a bed, in the midst of an orgy, eating peeled grapes while Rome burns. Or, to update the image, one may think of a drug addict devoting his or her life to getting high. Hedonists, in this popular understanding of the term, are regularly taken to be people without moral seriousness. How is the pursuit of *pleasure* a moral objective?

But remember we are talking about hedonism as a moral theory. The moral view known as hedonism is quite sophisticated, and thus it is far removed from the popular image of the pleasure-seeker. So let's highlight a few important components of hedonism as a moral theory. First, according to hedonism, pleasure is good and pain is bad, no matter who experiences them. Consequently, the pain of puppies is morally relevant, and the pleasures of one's friends, too. Perhaps more important, the hedonist claims that the pain even of one's enemies is bad, and their pleasure good. This suggests a further thought. The world is in a better moral condition overall when there are more experiences of pleasure and fewer experiences of pain. This suggests that we should act to promote pleasure and reduce suffering. So hedonists often hold that people have moral duties to follow laws, help those in need, respect people's privacy, and even be polite because these actions contribute to the greater happiness and reduce suffering. The hedonist view, then, would recommend against selfish pleasure-seeking and prescribe that each of us must strive to be moral caretakers of all sentient creatures. We must act in ways that take into account the suffering and happiness of everyone.

We can capture the intuition driving another secular ethical view by asking: What makes it wrong to lie? In lying, one deliberately misleads another by pretending to say something one believes true but instead saying what one does not believe is true. Because there is the general rule that one tells the truth, the person on the receiving end of a lie takes the liar's testimony as sincere and is thereby misled. The reason that lying is wrong is that it is a conflicted action. On the one hand, the liar must think that it is acceptable to lie—he or she is lying, after all. On the other hand, for the lie to be effective (for the other person to be deceived), lying must be wrong—people must be expected to tell the truth. That is, if lying were acceptable, then it would be impossible to deceive anyone with a lie. The moral perspective of a liar, then, is incoherent.

This test of the coherence of moral perspectives on many actions can explain their wrongness. Stealing is wrong because it treats ownership as something both acceptably ignored and protected (at first when something belongs to another, but later when it belongs to the thief). Hypocrisy is wrong because one holds that all should follow some specified plan of action, but then one doesn't follow it oneself. What arises from this consistency test is that we have roles to play in our society and in our interpersonal interactions that we must see as our duty to perform simply in virtue of the incoherence of wanting to do otherwise. This outlook is called *deontology* (from the Greek, *deon*, which means "duty"). It, too, was a widely recognized theory in Rome, held by the Stoics, and it was developed in the eighteenth century by German philosopher Immanuel Kant. It is widely recognized that the deontological outlook is highly formalized and has a tendency to be stark in its outlook for the good life and happiness (the short answer: doing one's duty). However, the view incorporates the remarkably powerful insight that there is a close connection between the demands of ethical life and the rational demands of consistency.

Let us turn our attention to a third ethical viewpoint. We can capture the intuition driving it by asking: Why is it good that children grow up strong, healthy, and smart? Why do we want to be happy? It seems that we don't desire our own flourishing or that of others for the sake of any other good. Happiness may bring with it many other good things, but we would desire it even if we alone could have it. It seems that the flourishing of a human being—the bringing to fruition of all (or at least a critical mass of) a person's intellectual, physical, and social capacities— is a good thing in and of itself.

Knowledge, for example, is an instrument for attaining many other things. Knowledge is power, as Francis Bacon observed, and it allows us to anticipate and control our environment. But our understanding of the world or our comprehension of some fact is also valuable in itself. Knowledge is a fulfillment of our intellectual capacities. Gracefulness is often a key to many other good things, perhaps the admiration of others. But gracefulness is also a good thing in and of itself as a perfection of our physical capacities. Fairness may bring with it stability and harmony, but it is good for its own sake as well. It is a completion of one's social development to recognize and be able to ensure that people get what they deserve.

This view that moral norms are grounded in the development of human excellence is often called *eudaimonism* (from the Greek *eudaimonia*, which means "happiness" or "fulfillment"), or *virtue-ethics*. Aristotle first developed the idea, and many of those who thought there was a Natural Law that reflected Divine Law, such as Thomas Aquinas, argued that the view was consistent with divine morality. But consistency goes only so far. On our sketch here, it seems clear that a good deal of the descriptions of developing human capacities into virtues can be done without recourse to mentioning God and His commands. Virtue ethics has had a long tradition as being a form of theological ethics, but there is nothing intrinsic to the notion of virtue or human excellence that requires that God be invoked.

One final take on nonreligious ethics can be captured by the puzzle as to how and when a lie can be justified. Is a lie to save a friend's feelings justified? A lie to save a life? Or take another familiar puzzle: We ought not to steal and we ought to provide for our children, but what should we do when we can provide for our children only by theft? These puzzles are fairly simple, but compelling answers that could command the assent of everyone are very difficult to find. The duty not to harm and the duty to be truthful can conflict. And when they do, it is not clear which duty should yield to the other. And the same goes for the duties of promoting human flourishing and respecting property. The goods behind these conflicting duties do not match up neatly so that we can see which one is the most important. The answers aren't easy to discern, but it nevertheless seems that there are right and wrong answers, or at least that there are some answers that are morally better than others. Telling your grandmother that she looks nice when she doesn't seems morally preferable to telling her the truth. Alternately, there are times for brutal honesty: often the incompetent need the truth about their ineffectiveness revealed to them.

Values come in a wide variety of forms. The good life is full of various and unruly good things, and sometimes they not only conflict but do so in ways that can be resolved only in the same messy ways that they came into conflict in the first place. *Pluralism* is the view that objective values come in a wide and messy variety. There is not one source of values but a plurality; thus, there are objective goods that compete with each other for our allegiance. Sometimes these values are in tension, and their proper resolutions are not easy to explain. Sometimes it is more important to tell the truth, and sometimes it is more important to respect people's feelings. What makes the difference? Often, we appeal to the specific *contexts* of the decisions; we say that some situations call for brutal honesty, others for considerate prevarication. And, as British philosopher W. D. Ross noted, sometimes we can't explain our decision in any principled way precisely because our choices are *between principles*. It is something that can only be left to good judgment. Ross says:

> The moral convictions of thoughtful and well-educated people are the data of ethics just as sense-perceptions are the data of natural science. (1930: 41)

Sometimes all we have to go on in moral conflicts are our moral intuitions—our considered sense of right and wrong. The job of moral theory is to work out the least contradictory set of moral principles that are agreeable to people who have thought hard about the issues. This is not to say that the answers are made "right" by our intuitions. The point is not that good and bad are what we—or some panel of alleged moral experts, or the majority of people—say they are. Rather, the claim is that sometimes we can do no better than to try to coordinate our best and most reflectively held moral judgments.

VII. LESSONS FROM NONRELIGIOUS MORAL THEORIES

There are a few lessons to be drawn from our admittedly swift and partial dash through secular moral theory. The first is that though our sketches are incomplete, they each seem plausible as far as they go. And if that's the case, then it's possible to explain moral goodness without recourse to God. We can do right-and-wrong talk without any God talk. The point, of course, is to show what we'd earlier called *the foundational claim* (either ethics comes from God and is objective and binding, or ethics comes from fleeting interests and is then subjective and non-binding) is *false*. There are *many* objective, binding, and nontheistic accounts of morality. It is possible not only to be good without God but also to develop accounts of the objectivity of morality that have no need of Him.

The second lesson is one of the central themes of this book: You can hold that someone else is wrong, in error, mistaken, and so on without thinking that he or she is stupid, incorrigible, malicious, or downright evil. All four of the secular ethical theories we've outlined here are exclusive of one another. This means that the truth of any of them entails that the others are false. Consider: Hedonists hold that the source of right and wrong is the proper balancing of pleasures and pains; deontologists hold that the source of moral obligation is in one's duty and the intelligibility of one's actions; virtue ethicists take moral goodness to be a feature of human fulfillment; and pluralists hold that there is perhaps an unlimited variety of sources of goodness. To adopt any of these theories is to hold that the other theories are false. But it is important to note that hedonists do not generally think that because the deontologist has the wrong moral theory, the deontologist is morally corrupt. Pluralists do not have to hold that those who think there is only one source of value are awful human beings. And to repeat, we, the authors, disagree about which of the four theories has advantage over the others. But neither of us has consequent worries about the other's capacity to be a responsible and sincerely moral person.

And there's the rub. It is possible to disagree with someone about an ethical question or even about the ultimate source of moral value without that holding the person with whom you disagree is untrustworthy or evil. Secular ethicists do it all the time. Religious believers do it all the time when they argue with those who disagree with them about how to interpret some lesson in the holy texts. And Paul did it when he recognized that the pagan Romans and Greeks could be moral despite the fact that they worshipped "false" gods. And so, now, why is it that this consideration is commonly not paid to *atheists*? We have argued against the common thought that God is necessary to ground or underwrite morality. We have also argued that atheists can hold that morality is objective. And much of what we have said shows that atheists and religious believers can share many of the same judgments about right and wrong and good and evil. So there is no justification at all for the popular view that atheists cannot be moral. Honest religious believers have to give up that old, tired canard.

CHAPTER FIVE

A MORAL CASE FOR ATHEISM

We have now cleared away the most common misconception of atheism, namely, that atheists are incapable of being moral or of recognizing objective right and wrong. We have shown thus far that there's nothing in atheism that would require a rejection of morality or the adoption of the view that morality is not objective. So atheists and religious believers can agree on central questions of moral theory. That's progress.

In the current chapter, we will present our case for nonbelief. Although we will have occasion to revisit some of the classical philosophical objections to God's existence, our case will draw primarily upon *moral* considerations against religious belief. Specifically, we will press two arguments. First, we shall examine the problem that the existence of persistent evil poses for certain popular varieties of religious belief; we will argue that atheism permits a morally proper attitude toward evil, whereas religious belief tends to dampen one's moral response. Second, we will revisit a line of thought associated with twentieth-century British philosopher Bertrand Russell according to which there is something immoral in the very thought that there exists something entitled to be worshipped by rational creatures; we shall argue that the actions and attitudes associated with worship are morally pernicious, since they are rooted in an abdication of moral autonomy.

We repeat once again that our aim here is not to produce a knock-

:heism. Serious religious believers will find much to
ie following pages. But that's precisely the point. We are
te reasonable debate over these matters between reli-
gious ᴜᴇ..ᴇᴠ.._ ᴨd atheists. To repeat, we are not trying to persuade religious believers to become atheists; rather, we aspire to convince religious
believers that atheists can—and often do—reject religious belief on the
basis of the kinds of moral reasons that religious believers tend to hold
are unavailable to the atheist. Put otherwise, we aim not to prove that
atheism is true and religious belief false, but that atheism must be seen
by the religious believer as *reasonable* and *moral*. The result of the
chapter, then, will be not that religious belief is ungrounded or foolish
but rather that the religious believer has reason to regard at least some
varieties of atheism as motivated by recognizably sound and compelling
moral considerations. It is still possible for the religious believer to
regard the atheist as seriously mistaken but nonetheless reasonable and
thus deserving of respectful engagement.

I. THE PROBLEM OF EVIL

Let's suppose there is a God who is all-good, all-powerful, and all-
knowing. Let's also suppose that this God created the world and main-
tains a keen interest in it. Why then does the world contain so much
evil? As He is all-powerful, God has the power to stop or prevent it. As
He is all-knowing, He knows it exists. As He is all-good, He must see fit
to eradicate evil. Yet evil persists. Why?

This is the problem of evil in a nutshell. The persistence of evil poses
a particularly pressing quandary for people who believe in the God
described above because it presents a problem that they themselves face
regularly in their own lives. After the attacks on 9/11, the 2004 tsunami

in Southeast Asia, and Hurricane Katrina, religious figures wrestled with the issue publicly, and many like-minded religious believers listened intently hoping for some words to make sense of both a world where awful things happen to innocent people and a God who appears to allow those things to happen.

But the answers these public figures provided were shockingly weak. In fact, they were hardly answers at all. To take one case in point, Billy Graham, when addressing the Episcopal National Cathedral on the National Day of Prayer and Remembrance after 9/11, openly asked why God permits suffering. Graham then conceded:

> I have to confess that I really do not know the answer totally, even to my own satisfaction. I have to accept by faith that God is sovereign, and He's a God of love and mercy and compassion in the midst of suffering.[1]

Later, in responding to Hurricane Katrina, Graham expressed similar sentiments:

> Whenever any disaster like this strikes, we often ask ourselves why. Why did God let this happen? I have been asked that question hundreds of times, and I have to confess that I do not know the full answer. . . . Job in the Bible asked the same question thousands of years ago, and his only answer was that God's ways are often beyond our understanding, and yet He is sovereign and He can still be trusted. The Bible says evil is a mystery. Someday we will understand, but not now.[2]

The problem of evil is thus not some new consideration that the atheist pulls out of his or her hat. The problem of evil arises because evil is a problem for us all. Evil presents a problem that religious believers such as Graham already recognize as a serious difficulty confronting their religious commitments, and as a momentous conundrum that must be grappled with. Evil must be responded to. Atheists and religious believers agree about this much: If there's a God of the kind described above, it is difficult to explain how there could be evil. More progress.

In this section, we'll try to make it clear how serious the problem of evil is. We will argue that the traditional responses to the problem of evil are generally inadequate, even when assessed by religious believers' own standards. So we will begin by presenting an inventory of the arguments religious believers use to respond to the problem of evil, and we will highlight the ways in which each argument fails. We will then argue that belief in God provides a positive obstacle to those who recognize the need to act against evil.

Another thing to note as we launch into our discussion of the problem of evil is that it provides one of the most popular atheist arguments against belief in God. The fact that atheists are concerned about evil contradicts the popular picture of the atheist as an immoralist. The atheist takes evil to provide a *moral argument* against belief in God. Contrary to the slur we encountered in the previous chapter—the atheist has no moral outlook—the argument from evil reveals the atheist to be the one with clear moral conviction.

Let's begin. The problem of evil starts with a familiar analysis of God's nature. The basic thought is that if God exists, He has all the requisite omniattributes. He is omnipotent, omniscient, and omnibenevolent. That is, with respect to power, knowledge, and goodness, He is perfect. And perfection here means that He lacks nothing that could make Him better in any of these respects. He is *all*-powerful, *all*-knowing, and *all-good*. Were He anything less, He would be a defective God—that is, no God at all. Thus, so long as He is, He has these three omniproperties. Also, such a being, were He to make a world, would make a perfectly good one. He would have the power to make such a world, He would know how to do it, and His supreme moral goodness would require Him to *want* to make such a world. And God indeed made a world. He made *this* world.

But alas this world that God made is clearly not perfectly good. In fact, this world has not just a few imperfections, it contains numerous, shocking, abhorrent evils. Common evils in the world are so horrific that we'd rather not detail them. Yet, to press the argument from evil, we've got to explain what we're talking about. If religious believers *do* have an answer to the problem of evil, they shouldn't blink when they hear stories of infant rape in South Africa, the suffering of those who died or lost loved ones in the attacks on 9/11, the death of toddlers in the rushing seawater of the tsunami in Southeast Asia, or the excruciating suffering of infants battling any one of the fatal diseases that afflict the newborn. The question, then, is Billy Graham's question: How God could allow such things?

II. FOUR THEODICIES

The problem of evil arises because it seems that religious believers are committed to a set of beliefs that does not hang together. We can capture this set with the following propositions:

1. God exists and is omnibenevolent, omniscient, and omnipotent.
2. God made the world.
3. If God made the world, it would be perfectly good.
4. There is evil in the world.
5. Worlds with evil are not perfectly good.

Again, God *could* have made a world without evil. And yet He didn't. Moreover, He *knew* what kind of world He was making. He *deliberately* made a world in which terrible, horrid, unconscionable evil regularly befalls even the most innocent among us. He *chose* to make a world filled with evil. Why?

Theodicy is the term used by philosophers and theologians to refer to the project of rendering God's existence consistent with persistent evil. A theodicy is an attempt to explain how God could justifiably allow evil and suffering in the world. Traditional theodicies endorse statements 1, 2, and 3. It's easy to see why. Rejecting 1 or 3 runs counter to the thought that God is perfect, and 2 is a condition for or at least part of a package of commitments necessary for God's relevance to us.

One traditional theodicy denies statement 4 and holds that evil is an illusion. St. Augustine, for example, famously contended that evil does not exist, but is merely the "privation of being" (1998: XII.7). Baruch Spinoza, alternatively, argued that humans can recognize value only in terms of themselves and their interests—we mistake inconveniences or things counter to our tastes for evils (1989: Book IV). According to Spinoza, there is no such thing as evil itself. A more general version of this thought has it that evil is merely *apparent*, and never real; it is the result of our feeble human perspective of the world. The thought continues that were we able to see the world from God's perspective, we'd see the world in its full perfection. We'd see that nothing is evil.

This strikes us as an especially odd theodicy. Its strategy for explaining evil is simply to explain evil away! It says that we merely need to change our perspective on the world; we only need to say that evil doesn't really exist. But unfortunately things aren't that simple. Return to our earlier examples. The consequences of infant rape are certainly real. The suffering is real. People's lives are destroyed. The rapes themselves, surely, are real; if they weren't, they wouldn't have consequences. So it's unclear what we're denying when we say there's no evil, but there is rape and all its consequent horror. We don't need anything more than that horror for there to be evil.

Now Augustine and Spinoza, and those that follow them, may be correct to think that there is no such thing as evil itself. But the argument from evil does not depend on there being evil in any *special* sense, whatever that might mean. We're talking about the evils of infant rape and drowning toddlers, and surely the world would be a morally better world without these things. To follow Spinoza in casting our concerns regarding evil as mere complaints is to fail to recognize the actual horrors that befall people; in fact, it is to diminish—perhaps deny—the moral significance of human suffering. This is obviously not a promising defense of God.

Another theodicy denies statement 5. It says that the evil in the world is a necessary means for greater goods to arise. On this line, Irenaeus, an early Christian theologian, and John Hick, a contemporary theologian, have argued that the evils in the world contribute to the production of good. For example, unpleasant experiences contribute to character building (think of boot camp). Without these evils, certain goods would not be attainable. Evils exist because they are necessary for there to be certain goods. So a world with evil in it might yet be a morally better world than a world without evil. Perhaps this is a morally perfect world after all.

This theodicy prompts three challenges. First, it's not clear that all evils can be understood in the same way. Yes, some evils do seem necessary for the attainment of certain greater goods. We take bad-tasting medicine for the sake of defeating disease, we endure the pain of exercise for the sake of attaining health, and so on. But not all evils work this way. It's not clear that all evils are necessary to attain some greater good. Examples are easy to imagine. Indeed, it's all too easy. What good comes of an infant rape? What greater good is accomplished by toddlers drowning in rushing seawater? Can the intense suffering of a child combating spina bifida be plausibly regarded as a necessary measure for character building?

Second, even if one concedes that good things somehow do come of these terrible episodes, it is unclear that the greater goods *justify* the evils. Almost any commonsense moral view acknowledges that sometimes the ends do not justify the means. That is, it is commonly thought that there are some means that it would be wrong to employ, even in the pursuit of great goods. In moral evaluation, we do not look simply to what someone has achieved; we also evaluate the means employed to produce the result. The view we're considering holds that God uses the lives of toddlers to bring about a supposedly greater good. But if God is a perfectly good being, shouldn't He draw the line at drowning toddlers, regardless of the goods thereby achieved? Shouldn't He recognize that there are some means that are morally inappropriate and thus unavailable to Him, even in His pursuit of great goods?

Third, even if evil is necessary for there to be certain goods, and even if the achievement of those goods *justifies* the evil means God employs, we must ask why God *must* employ evil means to accomplish these goods. As He is all-powerful and all-knowing, He must be able to achieve those same moral results without having to drown children. That is, God's omnipotence means that God is able to achieve any good without employing evil means. And if He's omniscient, He knows how to do this. So, assuming that the Southeast Asian tsunami was necessary for God to achieve some greater good, why did He allow children to drown? The problem of evil remains unsolved.

Another theodicy accepts statements 1 through 5 but denies that they are inconsistent. Those who take this route contend that evil in the world is not God's doing but is caused by human freedom. This is usually called the *free-will defense.* It runs as follows: God created a world where moral goodness is a possibility, and such possibilities also entail the possibility of evil. As moral goodness is not attainable without freedom, we must be equally free to choose evil rather than good. So the world's evils are consequences of human freedom. Or more precisely, the human *abuse* of freedom.[3]

There are three problems with the free-will defense. First, the free-will defense doesn't speak at all to the evil associated with tsunamis, hurricanes, and spina bifida. It may provide an answer to the question of why there is *moral evil* (the evil that people do to each other), but it cannot provide an answer to the question of why there is *natural evil* (the evil that results from disease, disasters, accidents, and other incidents that are ironically called *acts of God*). Perhaps it's true that there are murders because humans abuse their free will. Perhaps it's true that a lot of the suffering in the world is due to humans behaving badly. And maybe it would be a worse world were God to intervene whenever anyone tries to act wrongly against another. But sadly that doesn't explain all the evil there is in the world.

Why does God allow there to be spina bifida? Suppose you discovered a cure for spina bifida but refused to share it with the world, resolving instead to simply allow thousands upon thousands of children to suffer with the disease every day. How could it possibly be good to do that? Wouldn't withholding the cure make you a bad person? Wouldn't it be morally appropriate to say that you're morally blameworthy? Arguably you're even *responsible* for the suffering of thousands of children. Only a moral villain would withhold the cure for a terrible disease. Yet God is in the position that we just imagined. He knows how to cure spina bifida. Indeed, He doesn't need to *cure* it; He can simply will the disease out of existence. Yet He doesn't. And as a consequence, children suffer terribly. It's hard to see how this could be necessary for preserving free will. It seems then that on the free-will defense God is a moral villain.

Second, there is a conceptual problem with the free-will defense. The free-will defense is based on the assumption that being free is inconsistent with God guaranteeing that one always chooses the good. But why couldn't God create a world of free and perfectly good beings, ones who always freely choose to do the right thing? He could have, and it seems that He should have. If He couldn't have, then it seems that either (a) God is not omnipotent, or (b) God is not perfect because *He's* either not free or not perfectly good. The thought is that God is perfectly good *and* is free. So it must be possible to be free and to always freely choose the good. Take Jesus. If he wasn't free, he wouldn't be human, and if he wasn't supremely good, he wasn't God. By hypothesis, Jesus was both free and good, so it must be possible for there to be free creatures that always choose the good. Free will is compatible with perfect goodness. So why didn't God make us perfectly good?

The third problem with the free-will defense is the problem of negligence. Let's consider a simple example. You're at a restaurant and you mistakenly leave your wallet on the table. As you walk away, the waiter sees the abandoned wallet and quickly pockets it. He has stolen your wallet and thus has certainly chosen to do something wrong. But let's suppose further that another guest at the restaurant witnesses the waiter stealing the wallet. Assume of course that the witness knows that the wallet does not belong to the waiter and knows that stealing is wrong; assume also that the witness could easily stop the waiter from stealing the wallet by simply calling your attention to the fact that you had mistakenly left it behind. It seems clear to us that in this case the witness would be wrong not to stop the waiter, not to call your attention to the fact that you had left your wallet behind. Indeed, if the witness doesn't do what he or she can to stop the waiter from taking your wallet, he or she is not only negligent but also complicit in the crime. Of course, he or she may be respecting the thief's freedom in not intervening, but in doing this, he or she nonetheless is morally responsible to some degree for the wrong that has been done to you. By analogy, on the free-will defense, it is hard to see God as anything other than complicit with the most heinous crimes. He sees them being committed, He knows that they are moral crimes, yet He does nothing to stop them. The free-will defense requires us to think of God as an idle bystander, perfectly willing to allow evil to occur simply for the sake of preserving free will. But non-interventionism is not clearly required for preserving free will. And in any case, it seems to be an immoral policy when it comes to serious evils.

The final theodicy we will consider is what may be called the *biblical solution*. The previous theodicies we have considered derive solely from the human intellect; they represent attempts to employ human reason to render God's existence consistent with worldly evil. The assumption behind these theodicies is that human reason is sufficient to work out the problems of theology. The alternative represented by the biblical solution involves a turn away from human intellectual capacities and toward revealed truths.

Those who employ the biblical solution claim that the human condition is hamstrung by feeble human reason. We cannot make progress on the hard questions of theology by exercising our rational powers. Those powers are too weak. So we need help from outside. The basic thought driving the biblical solution is that the Bible tells us God, in fact, *did* make the best world: Eden. But then *we* messed it up; call that *the Fall*. Consequently, in this fallen world, things are out of sync with the good. Thus there are tsunamis, hurricanes, spina bifida, and other tragedies and horrors. These are all consequences of the Fall. We broke the world, so we have to live in it. That's why there's so much evil.

The biblical solution goes further to claim that some evil events are not simply consequences of the Fall. These events are God's machinations, steps in God's plan for the world, results of God's actions. Consider Job's suffering. God's reasons are incomprehensible to Job; they comprise a wisdom Job simply cannot grasp. But the events that unfold are nevertheless in accordance with God's will. They are part of His work in the world. And for that reason, the biblical solution contends, they are just.

Now, it is important to notice that once it is claimed that this is a *fallen* world, many premises driving the problem of evil are denied. What do denizens of a fallen world deserve? Do they deserve wealth, health, pleasure, joy, and comfort? No. They deserve punishment and ultimately death. On the biblical solution, it is only at the end of things that good will be done. In the meantime, we must endure. The doctrine of the Fall is thus a denial of the thought that the suffering in the world is evil. In a fallen world, all suffering is *deserved*. By way of summary, we might capture the biblical solution in the following three theses:

I. *Revelationism.* Human reason cannot make progress on the problem of evil without the aid of revelation.
II. *Fallen world–ism.* The world is fallen, broken, and its denizens not only are also fallen, but they deserve the discomforts that come with living in a fallen world.
III. *Mysterianism.* God acts on and intervenes in the world, but His purposes are beyond our comprehension.

There are four problems with the biblical solution. First is the problem of displaced moral responsibility. We—you, us, everyone else presently alive, and the great majority of people who have ever lived— didn't have anything to do with the Fall. *We weren't even there.* Neither were those children who drowned in the tsunami. So why do *we* deserve punishment? Even if it is true that Adam and Eve broke the perfect world of Eden, it is unjust for God to make us live in it. Moreover, if God is morally perfect and has compassion for us, it seems He should have forgiven us by now. Seriously, who holds a grudge that long? It seems excessive for God to punish generation after generation for a slip in judgment, even a serious slip.

Second is the problem of unequal moral responsibility. If we all deserve punishment because of the Fall—if, that is, we are all to be held responsible for the same immoral act—then the punishment should be evenly distributed. As none of us now is more to blame for the Fall than any other living person, we should all get an equal amount of the suffering that is the result. But evils are not equally distributed in this world. Indeed, they're *not even close* to being equitably distributed. Even if it is conceded that we all deserve punishment for the Fall, the inequity is clearly unjust.

Third is the problem of selective hiddenness. Although it may sound impressively deep to say in the face of evil and suffering that we can't judge God or that His ways are incomprehensible to us, such claims contradict much of what religious believers frequently claim about God. For example, religious believers say that God is good. They assert that He is omniscient. They praise Him for His wisdom, mercy, patience, and beneficence. They urge us all to trust in Him. They affirm that He loves even the worst of us, that He wants to take care of us, and that His heart is always open. They claim that He will save us. And so on. In short, religious believers typically claim to know a great deal about God and His nature.

The biblical solution renders all these claims problematic. One cannot affirm that God is good, wise, omniscient, and the rest but then respond to evil by saying that God is inherently mysterious. If God is incomprehensible to us, then we should not assert that He is good, beneficent, just, wise, merciful, and loving. But religious believers insist on these claims about God's nature. Indeed, they often appeal to God in their explanations of everyday events; they thank God when good things happen and ask for God's intervention in various affairs. Yet when evil occurs, they turn mysterian and say that God is unintelligible. This strikes us as dishonest. If God is indeed unintelligible, then He cannot be properly credited for the good in the world. If, by contrast, He is properly credited with the good in the world, then He is not unintelligible to us, and the mysterian component of the biblical solution is false. It seems to us, then, that the biblical solution is no answer to the problem of evil at all.

Fourth, and finally, is the problem of interpretation. The biblical solution is posited on the claim that God reveals Himself through the Bible. God speaks through the Bible by means of revelation. A revelation is a special kind of message, and as with any message, revelation requires interpretation. In interpreting messages, we need to appeal to our background beliefs about the source of the message and its purpose. Among the questions we must ask are: Is the person sincere? Is this message for *me*? Is the message to be taken literally or metaphorically? Is the person who sent it being sarcastic or speaking in hyperbole? What is the person trying to accomplish with the message?

The biblical solution asks us to take God's moral attributes as mysterious, beyond our comprehension, and so on, but then takes His communicative acts to be perfectly intelligible. Put otherwise, the biblical solution requires one to say that one has no idea what God is up to when He lets babies drown, but one knows for sure what He's up to when He says that Jesus is His son. Thus our question: If God lets babies die for no discernable reason, how do we know that He's not speaking metaphorically in revelation? For that matter, how do we know He's not lying? If letting innocent babies die in a torrent of rushing seawater is acceptable to God, then why should He have any qualms about committing lesser moral offenses, such as lying? And if the religious believer's response is to appeal to *mystery* or *faith* or *grace* or any such thing, we simply say again that the biblical solution really offers no answer to the problem of evil.

III. ATHEISM AND EVIL

As a response to evil, the atheist rejects God's existence. Atheists hold that God's existence and perfection is inconsistent with all the suffering and evil in the world. The argument runs as follows: If God exists, and the world contains all the evil that it does, then God is unjust. But because the very notion of God entails that He is the very best, most perfect being, it follows that God cannot exist. Consider: If He exists, then He's unjust. But if He's unjust, then He isn't perfect. And if He isn't perfect, He can't be God. So God doesn't exist.

It bears repeating at this point that our discussion of the problem of evil should make some progress in rehabilitating the popular image of the atheist. Remember that the common view holds that atheists are immoralists. It is often claimed that, as they reject God's guidance, atheists have no ethical vision or principle and no moral clarity or seriousness. Some, including Ravi Zacharias, go further to claim that atheists have killed God as the source of value, and so turn to killing everything valuable around them in the form of relativism and liberalism. And some go even further. Dinesh D'Souza contends that "atheism is motivated not by reason but by a kind of cowardly moral escapism" (2007: xvii). According to this popular image, atheism is a form of cultural suicide. When God's commandments are not respected or acknowledged, people have given up on God. And, as Carl F. H. Henry contends, God, in turn, will give up on them.

But the argument from evil not only provides a rational argument against the existence of God, it also affords the atheist a level of moral clarity and seriousness that religious believers typically lack. The argument from evil is a *moral argument* against the existence of God, and its upshot is that atheists take moral norms more seriously than many religious believers do. In raising the problem of evil, the atheist is the one who calls injustice by its real name. By contrast, the religious believer, in his or her fidelity to his or her belief in God, loses the seriousness required for consistent moral judgment. Recall that many of the theodicies we canvassed earlier say that one has no idea what good God accomplishes by allowing infant rape or what God's ultimate moral rules are when He does not stop toddlers from being washed away in giant waves. These, certainly, should be reasons for religious believers to question their God's moral judgment. Yet religious believers offer excuses for God.

Note that our argument is not simply that atheists can be moral. The argument is rather that atheists are uniquely placed to be *consistently* moral. Recall that theodicy requires of religious believers that they make special moral exceptions for their God that one would not reasonably make for anyone else. Accordingly, theodicy requires believers to refrain from holding God to the moral principles that they most frequently claim are central to their religious conviction. To be clear, religious believers often claim to be committed to very admirable moral precepts: human life is inviolable, one must protect the vulnerable, one must fight against injustice, and so on. But then theodicy requires the religious believer to exempt God from these very requirements. Accordingly, each of the religious believer's moral precepts admits of an exception, namely, God.

By contrast, the atheists are steadfast in their moral commitments. For them, moral rules are moral rules, and nobody is exempt from these rules. We are all equals before the moral law. This point is significant. The strategy for all theodicies is to *rationalize* evil, to say that the evil in the world is part of God's plan, is all for the better, or is all an illusion. According to the theodicies we examined, the world is just fine as it is; everything is as it should be, morally speaking. Hence, there's no need for anyone to strive for change. The result of theodicy, therefore, is *moral quietism*, the view that all's well with the world. Quietism promotes *moral indifference*, the view that because all's well with the world, there's no need for anyone to exert moral effort in improving anything.

As a result, it is the religious believer, and not the atheist, who is driven to adopt an immoralist attitude. If all's well with the world and God is in charge, there's no need to fight injustice, to work to prevent suffering, or to protect the vulnerable. Again, the view of the religious believer is either that there is no evil in the world or, if indeed there is any evil, God will take care of it. For the religious believer, good and evil are someone else's business.

Hence, it is simply an *error* when religious believers and political commentators such as Jim Wallis claim that their commitment to God's existence and goodness not only allows them to recognize evil but impels them to take steps to prevent or remedy it. Wallis contends that it is precisely *because* religion takes the problem of evil so seriously that religious believers must always be suspicious of too much concentrated power—politically and economically—either in totalitarian regimes or in huge multinational corporations that have more wealth and power than many governments. On Wallis's view, the existence of evil makes religious believers strong proponents of freedom, liberty, and democracy. Wallis supports these not because people are so good, but because they often are bad and therefore need clear safeguards and strong systems of checks and balances to avoid the dangerous accumulations of power and wealth.

We, the authors, are also committed to freedom, liberty, and democracy. Our question for Wallis is how these commitments could follow from the view that, thanks to God, the world is precisely as it should be. To put the point differently, the proposed theodicies support a range of morbid political attitudes. Consider: If you deny that there is evil in the world, then there is no need to punish infant rape. If you believe that the evil in the world contributes to our moral improvement, then there is no need to prevent children from being swallowed by a rushing wave of seawater. In fact, if everything that occurs contributes to our moral improvement, perhaps we should *promote* evils. The same should go for Wallis's political commitments. Why prevent poverty or tyranny if it improves the souls of those who suffer it? After all, God Himself does not prevent these things, and He is morally perfect! If one adopts the free-will defense, then all preventive measures curtail the freedom that God Himself refuses to curtail. If God judges it more important to respect the rapist's freedom, then who are we to step in? If one accepts the biblical solution, then one should be happy about the misery in the world because all misery is just; everyone gets what he or she deserves.[4]

The problem of evil, then, not only exposes a serious problem for those who want to assert that God exists. Once they turn to any of the standard theodicies, religious believers are confronted with a deeper problem. In order to explain how evil is compatible with God's existence, the available theodicies force the religious believer to commit to moral beliefs that are highly suspect, such as that there is really no evil in the world, that intense suffering is necessary to improve our moral character, or that a world that features tsunamis and spina bifida is a morally better world than one without these things. As we have suggested, theodicy does not only require religious believers to adopt questionable moral beliefs; it also promotes the debilitating moral attitudes of quietism and indifference in the face of serious evil. Theodicies require religious believers to grow as heartless as the God they worship.

In the end, it is hard to resist British mathematician W. K. Clifford's thought: "If men were no better than their religions, the world would be a hell indeed" (1999: 104).

That was harsh. But we have put things very starkly for a reason. We want to show that atheists can indeed wield moral judgments, and that those moral judgments can be cornerstones for rejecting belief in God. Furthermore, we want to punctuate that it is the moral seriousness of facing evil in the world that impels the atheist to reject God's existence.

On our view, belief in God is an impediment to clear moral thinking and effective action in eradicating evil and promoting justice. If you think we are wrong, that's fine. We welcome your objections. But notice that to engage with us on the problem of evil, you will have to engage in an argument about the nature and demands of morality. This means that you will first have to admit that we, the atheists, are not libertine immoralists looking to overthrow the constraints of objective morality. Our atheism is the product of the same moral commitments that many religious believers embrace. The challenge we present is that of reconciling your everyday moral judgments about good and evil and right and wrong—judgments that we regard as thoroughly sound—with your belief in God.

IV. ATHEISM AND CONSOLATION

Dinesh D'Souza asks, "where is atheism when bad things happen?" His claim is that, despite the fact that atheism offers a simple response to the problem of evil, it can provide no consolation to those who suffer those evils. According to D'Souza, that is a job only for those who believe in God, a job that atheists are *unable* to perform. D'Souza argues:

> [S]uffering doesn't wreck minds; it wrecks hearts. When I get sick, I don't want a theory to explain it; I want something that will make me feel better. Atheism may have a better explanation for evil and suffering, but it provides no consolation for them. Theism, which doesn't have a good explanation, nevertheless offers a better way for people to cope with the consequences of evil and suffering. (2007: 274)

D'Souza concedes that evil is a mystery, but he defends belief in God on the ground that it alone offers consolation to the suffering. We find

D'Souza's position here utterly absurd. Suppose you are suffering from a serious and painful disease. What consolation is there in the thought that there is an all-good, all-powerful, and all-knowing God who presides over the world yet allows you to suffer? God could, of course, have prevented the disease and could now will the disease away. Yet He does nothing. Is *that* a *comforting* thought? Could such a thought possibly help those suffering evil to cope? Doesn't the thought that there is a God simply *add* to the horror? In fact, it seems to us that for those who believe in God, every instance of evil contains *two* moral tragedies: The first is the experience of suffering; the second is the fact that God could have intervened to prevent or lessen the suffering but has declined to do so. Far from offering consolation for evil, belief in God seems simply to multiply the injuries.

Perhaps D'Souza is claiming that, as a matter of fact, belief in God lessens the suffering. Perhaps his view is that belief in God indeed provides solace to those in distress. But this seems unconvincing to us. Remember the earlier quotations from Billy Graham. When tragedy occurs, people openly wrestle with the problem of evil. They struggle not only to cope with the tragedy—but to reconcile the fact that the tragedy occurred with their religious convictions. And if they are trying to answer the problem of evil, they *must* be troubled by it. Losing a child to a tsunami is a terrible thing to have to endure. Having to confront the additional realization that *God allowed it to happen* is a *further* source of suffering. Again, belief in God *adds* to our distress when we suffer, or even witness suffering. D'Souza is wrong again. Suffering plagues hearts *and* minds.

But there is something true in what D'Souza says. Atheism indeed provides no consolation in the face of suffering. We do not appeal to atheism as a source of solace or comfort. This is not because we reject the idea that those who are suffering should be left to fend for themselves.

The point is that when we seek to console someone who is suffering, God's existence or nonexistence is irrelevant. Solace is gained not from the belief in God or the claim that God has a plan. Rather, it comes from the support, care, friendship, and love of others. It comes from the assurance that human relationships exist that will endure through the period of suffering and help the person who is suffering cope with it. In fact, appeals to God's plan are often simply ways of assuring the person who is suffering that you will, indeed, help him or her cope. God, then, is really beside the point. At best, religious belief is a distraction away from the intimacy of relationship between people who care deeply for one another. At worst, it compounds the suffering by adding to the tragedy the extra insult of God's inaction.

To wrap up, many atheists have *moral* reasons for rejecting belief in God. The problem of evil is a familiar and crisp way to capture the thought that taking morality seriously leads one to deny of God's existence. But there is another kind of moral argument against religious belief, one that perhaps is less familiar to religious believers. But it seems to us to be an even more compelling moral argument for atheism. We call it the problem of worship.

V. THE PROBLEM OF WORSHIP

We have been using the term *religious belief* to refer to a certain cluster of views. Specifically, we have been focused thus far on the belief that God exists. And we have been working with a conception of God according to which God is the all-knowing, all-good, all-powerful creator of the world who stands apart from His creation but takes a keen interest in what goes on there. Let us now call this cluster of religious beliefs concerning God and His nature *theism*. In the first chapter of this book, we noted that the term *theism* is used in many different ways. That is true. But now we are stipulating that we will use the term in this specified way.

The commitments that constitute theism should have a familiar ring. Theism is, after all, the conception of God who is common to the Abrahamic religions, among many others. But there is one additional commitment of theism that comes along with the others but is often not discussed: *humans are obligated to worship God*.

The thought that God is the proper object of worship places limits upon how we interpret the other theistic commitments. There are different versions of theism, and these employ different interpretations of what it means for God to be all-powerful, omniscient, and a creator. However, despite these significant differences, every version of theism holds that God is entitled to our worship. This is the heart of theism. We will argue in this section that we *shouldn't* worship God. That we shouldn't worship God follows from a more general thesis for which we shall argue, namely, that *we shouldn't worship anything*. And if there's nothing that we should worship, then there is no God.

Importantly, here's another point of agreement between the kind of atheism we advocate and many popular forms of religious belief. We agree that if there is a God, we should worship Him. God, were He to exist, would be the proper object of worship. Now, the question is whether anything is the proper object of worship. And so we must ask what exactly it is for something to be a proper object of worship?

This much seems clear: If it's proper that God be worshipped, then creatures capable of worshipping ought to worship God. To be sure, not all creatures are capable of worship. Cats and dogs, for example, do not have the requisite capacities for worship. But humans do. Humans have the required rational capacities to be *moral agents*; we can recognize moral duties, express gratitude, feel shame and guilt, demand justice, act for the sake of satisfying moral obligations, and so on. So we might put the point like this: If God ought to be worshipped, then all things with the capacity for rationality and moral agency should worship God, and things without the capacity for rationality and moral agency are not required to worship God. Again, cats and dogs don't have to worship God because they can't worship anything; they do not have the capacity for worship. And because they do not have the capacity to reason and exercise moral agency, they can't be held responsible for what they do. Cats and dogs have no obligations at all.

But consider a different example. According to the common story, Satan does not worship anything. However, Satan nonetheless accepts all the other theistic commitments. He believes that God exists. He believes that God embodies all the omniattributes. He believes that God created the world, performs miracles, takes a keen interest in human lives, and so on. Yet Satan refuses to worship God. That's his sin.

Satan's sin reveals to us not only that we have an obligation *to* worship; his case also shows us something about what worship is. Satan has all the right beliefs about God, but this is not enough. He also is obligated to do certain things, to behave in a certain way, and even to have a proper attitude about God. And this is where he fails. In other words, worship involves having the proper *comportment* toward God. Satan is improperly deferential to God; he does not respond appropriately to God's presence, His nature, and His commands. Satan is insufficiently obedient to God, and thus he does not love Him.

The case of Satan is instructive. It shows that if indeed God is entitled to our worship, we are required to worship Him in a way that is *complete*. In other words, our relationship with God, if it is to be the *right kind* of relationship, must be *all-in*. God demands of us not only that we trust in Him or praise Him or love Him. He is entitled to the *greatest* trust, the *highest* praise, and *complete* love. And to trust, praise, and love Him to the highest degree is to do so unquestioningly and without qualification. To question whether God deserves our highest praise is to withhold our highest praise; to wonder whether God deserves our *greatest* trust is to withhold some degree of trust; to love God conditionally is to not love Him entirely. That is, to question—or even wonder—about what one owes God by way of trust, praise, and love is to fail to give God His due. It is to fall short of our obligation to worship Him. And that is to sin against Him.

This strikes us as a dubious requirement. Is it right to require that beings who are capable of reason and moral agency must submit unconditionally to another? Recall that the requirement of worship is restricted to those capable of recognizing the requirement. Once again, cats and dogs can't worship God because they don't have the intellect or moral agency to do so. We humans are required to worship precisely because of our rational moral agency. But now note what worship involves. In order to worship, we must abandon our rational moral agency. We must submit our judgment to that of another.

Let's back up for a moment. We have said that humans are capable of rational moral agency. This means that humans can respond rationally to moral reasons, considerations about what is right and wrong. That is, rational moral agents are creatures who are capable of thinking things through and doing what's right by their best lights. They are creatures who are capable of acting in ways that reflect their moral deliberations. Accordingly, rational moral agents can be held *morally responsible* for what they do. That means that they are properly blamed when they do wrong, and praised when they do what's right. Praise and blame are appropriate precisely because rational moral agents are *in control* of their actions; when rational moral agents are acting responsibly, their actions are manifestations of their reasoning.

This is why we do not regard cats and dogs as moral agents. To be sure, one might hold that cats and dogs have *moral standing*. This means simply that there are right and wrong ways in which one might treat a cat or a dog. But not everything that has moral standing is a moral agent. Dogs are incapable of moral reasoning. They cannot act for the sake of doing what's right. They can be *trained* to do good deeds, of course. But when a dog assists a blind person across a street, the dog is acting on the basis of its training. Humans are importantly different. We are capable of acting simply on the basis of our reasoning about what's right and wrong. Accordingly, when we do wrong, we can be held morally responsible for what we do. Consider, by contrast, an ill-behaved dog. Dogs are not subject to moral evaluation at all, even when they behave badly. Ill-behaved dogs require better training, not moral condemnation. When *we* behave badly, by contrast, we do wrong and thus deserve moral blame.

Now, if worship requires unquestioning and unqualified obedience, it seems that the only theologically acceptable free act we can perform is the act of submitting our lives to God. And once we submit to God, we must abdicate our capacity for independent moral judgment. Once again, if God deserves all-in trust, praise, love, and so on, then to question—or even to wonder about—any of His demands is to sin. Actions done independently of God's commands, even if they accord with what God commands, are nevertheless failures of obedience.

Perhaps it may help to think of this from the perspective of the perennial question of the meaning of life. A common thought expressed by religious believers is that we were made to adore God. Hence St. Anselm opened his *Proslogion* with the following address to God Himself: "I was made in order to see You" (1979: 112). This requires that we view ourselves as divine artifacts, each with a purpose assigned to us in advance by a divine maker, namely, God. We must view ourselves as players on a stage made by God for God. Questioning or resisting this assigned purpose is presumptuous to the point of sinfulness. On this view, there are no legitimate places for us to raise our objections to God. He has given us a job.

And who are we to question Him? Consider God's rebuke to Job when Job seemed to chafe at the thought that God could have stopped his suffering. God said, "Who is this whose ignorant words cloud my design in darkness?" (Job 38:2). Later, God expressed the thought more pointedly. "Dare you deny that I am just or put Me in the wrong so that you may be right?" (Job 40:7–8). Job, being who he is, kept his place. And, apparently, this is the right thing to do when dealing with God.

Now, it's one thing to view oneself as an instrument of a divine will in the sense that one has taken up the project or shouldered a burden on behalf of something one sees as worthwhile. One can certainly take up a cause, devote one's life to it, and thus see oneself as an instrument of that cause. But it is another thing to view oneself as an instrument of a divine will because one has been *forced* to adopt that role. The first is the view of a free devotee; the latter is the view of a slave. One may, like Job, chafe at one's bonds, or one may accept them as inevitable. But either way, one is a slave.

Consider another analogy. Worshipping God, presumably, is a very intimate affair. If worship is *required* of us, then we have a moral obligation to be intimate with God. If we do not feel the pull of that intimacy, then we have morally failed in some deep way, and presumably we would deserve punishment. Now, under what conditions is it just to require of a person that she be intimate with another? There are many things wrong with the act of rape, but one of the things morally offensive about rape is that it is an act of *forced intimacy*. A person is forced into an intimate relationship with another who threatens violence for refusal. Intimacy, if genuine and worth the name, is something that is necessarily given freely; when intimacy is forced, bought, coerced, or induced in any other way, it is not really intimacy but a *perversion* of intimacy.

Imagine a powerful comedian who says, "Find my jokes funny, or I will beat you." There are of course many things odd about such a comedian, and we might even find the very thought of such a comedian funny. But one thing worth noting is that the comedian has failed to understand what it is to find a joke funny. One cannot be *forced* to find a joke funny. One can be forced to *laugh* at a joke. But forced laughter is not genuine laughter; it is counterfeit laughter. Counterfeit laughter is merely the producing of certain sounds; it does not express one's judgment that a given joke is funny. The fact is that the comedian cannot force you to find his or her jokes funny. He or she can at best force you to act as if you did. Finding a joke funny is not something that can be the result of a command or even an obligation.

The same is true with intimacy. Forced intimacy is fake intimacy, thus not intimacy at all. Those who are required to act in ways that typically would express intimacy are like the people feigning laughter at the comedian's jokes. They are not expressing genuine intimacy but rather are acting as if they felt an intimate relation with another. And those who feign intimacy because a powerful agent threatens punishment if intimacy is withheld are slaves of a sort.

Insofar as we see intimate devotion to God as an unconditional requirement that we must meet if we are to avoid serious punishment, our worship of Him is tainted. Compelled worship is forced intimacy. If God takes Himself to be *entitled* to be worshipped, if He takes it that humans are *required* to worship Him, He is like the comedian described above. His threat "worship Me or else" is not only conceptually confused about the nature of worship, it is immoral.

There surely are good reasons for submitting to or obeying authorities under certain conditions. For example, we submit to the cognitive authority of textbook writers, news reporters, and teachers. We believe what they say, and sometimes we even do as they say. We do this because they know things we do not know. In addition, we submit to the institutional authority of police officers, lawmakers, and governments because of the legitimacy of the institutions they represent. In every case of deference, we defer on the basis of our recognition that the institution or the person to whom we defer has a certain status that confers upon them *authority*. Importantly, in cases in which we submit to authority, we submit only conditionally. Submission is never all-in; authorities can always be questioned, and when necessary challenged or overturned.

When we submit to authority responsibly, we do so because we have judged that submission in the given case is morally appropriate. So if we must submit to God and worship Him, we should do so on the basis of recognizing Him to possess some special property that makes him worthy of worship. Call these properties *W-properties*. If we are obliged to view God as worthy of worship, then we must have reason to see some W-property that God has as making Him worthy of worship. Analogously, if there were people who demand our deference but have no credentials, not only would we have no obligation to defer to them, but it would be positively irresponsible for us to defer. Accordingly, unless God has some specifiable property that makes Him worthy of worship, then it would be irresponsible to worship Him.

And here is the problem. None of the properties that theism attributes to God amount to reasons to worship Him. In other words, theistic conceptions of God claim a lot about God's nature, but they specify no property of God that is a plausible W-property. To show this, we'll canvass a few of the divine attributes that are sometimes presented as W-properties. Then we will explain why those properties are not appropriate bases for the obligation to worship God.

One traditional theistic strategy is to start with the claim that God's essence entails His existence. (We encountered this claim in chapter 3 in our discussion of the Ontological Argument. Recall that the basic idea is that God is, by definition, a perfect being; and a perfect being must be an existing being, otherwise it would be less than perfect.) Perhaps the fact that it is necessarily the case that God exists is the source of His worshipability, the property in virtue of which we should worship Him. But note that simple truths of arithmetic are also necessarily true. We couldn't someday discover that two plus two equals five; it is necessarily the case that two plus two equals four. Necessary truths do not seem to us to provide a reason to worship. That it's necessarily true that God exists is not a W-property.

Perhaps we should worship God because of His other essential properties, what we earlier identified as the omniattributes. Does the fact that God is omniscient or omnipotent provide a reason to worship Him? We may certainly be *impressed* with God's power and knowledge. But these attributes do not impel worship. It seems to us that worshipping something specifically because of its power is problematic.[5] Furthermore, we find the idea of a God who knows our innermost thoughts less impelling of worship than paranoia. In fact, we think there may be an argument analogous to the problem of evil to be made at another time, roughly about *the problem of privacy,* which would contend that a perfectly just being would respect our privacy and hence would not be omniscient. In any case, omniscience and omnipotence are not W-properties.

Omnibenevolence seems to us to be the most promising candidate for being a W-property. That God is perfectly good seems to us to be a feature of God that perhaps deserves more than our deepest admiration. But it nonetheless seems excessive to say that because God is omnibenevolent, He must be worshipped. If God is morally superior to us, we should of course strive to live up to His example. But worship is a step beyond. Recall that worship requires us to *obey* God. The thought that God's omnibenevolence provides a compelling reason to strive to morally emulate God derives its force from the idea that God can be an object of our moral evaluation. Again, we are to be impressed with God's goodness and emulate it *because* we judge it to be superlative. But worship requires that we obey, not judge, God.

So neither God's necessary existence nor the theistic omniattributes count as W-properties. On the basis of what, then, does God deserve to be worshipped? Here's a thought. God created the world and everything in it, including us. Perhaps we are obligated to worship Him in recognition of all He has done for us. Were it not for Him, none of us would exist. So He deserves our thanks.

This line of thought raises the following problem. Giving thanks to God is different from worshipping Him. Even giving *really big thanks* is different from worship. Once again, giving thanks to God involves estimating how deserving God is of our thanks. And thus, in giving God really big thanks, we must judge how big a thanks He deserves. But once again, worshipping God is different from judging Him, even in cases in which we judge Him to be superlative. Thanking God is a way of judging Him. Consequently, it is not worship.

Maybe we should worship God simply because He tells us to. After all, He is God and He says we should worship Him. So we should, full stop. One wanting to take this thought a little further might add that the first two of the Ten Commandments are at the top of the list for a reason. God clearly thinks it's *really important* that we worship Him. So we should.

But the view that we should worship God simply because He says so gets everything backward. We began with the question of why we should worship God and do what He says. The answer we are considering claims that we should worship Him and do what He says *because* He says that we should worship Him and do what He says. But what's at issue is the status, or force, of God's pronouncements about what we should do! Even if He commands us to worship Him, it's not clear that His commands have any force until we can establish that He is properly regarded as an authority to whom we must submit.

Perhaps a different strategy is required. Let's go back to the omni-attributes. Maybe God is worth worshipping because He is omnibenevolent *and* He says that we should worship Him. As God is perfectly good, He is a reliable source of moral instruction. So when He tells us that we ought to do something, it is highly likely that it is true that we ought to do it. And, importantly, He says that we ought to worship Him. So we should.

This is an interesting argument. We've already debated that there is a moral problem with worship in that it undoes an agent's moral agency. An omnibenevolent being wouldn't require of moral agents that they abdicate their capacities for moral agency. An all-good God wouldn't treat rational creatures like that. But the argument we just sketched above raises a slightly different question. What kind of omnibenevolent being would *command* rational creatures to worship Him?

An analogy might help us grasp the issue. Let's say that Kate is exceptionally generous and deserves praise for her generosity. We may even suppose that Kate *expects* recognition for her generosity in the form of praise. But let's imagine that Kate doesn't get the praise she deserves. If in response to this she were to *demand* praise for generosity, we would have good reason to be disappointed in Kate. Kate may be generous and deserving of praise, but in *demanding* praise, she has revealed herself to be *petulant*. Consequently, Kate's virtues are not complete. Her generosity is still exceptional and deserving of praise, but she has shown herself to have a moral vice.

The fact that God commands us to worship Him places Him in Kate's ethical territory. Perhaps God is so great that He deserves to be worshipped. That does not entail that God can rightly demand that we worship Him. Furthermore, that God commands us to worship Him seems to concede that we really don't have reasons for worshipping Him after all. God commands us to worship Him. We ask, "Why?" He answers, "Because I say so." But what kind of reason is that? Accordingly, we're inclined to say that if God commands us to worship Him, we have very good reason *not* to.

Let's consider one further attempt to identify a sufficient reason to worship God. One may hold that one worships God for the sake of one's redemption; by worshipping God, one achieves salvation from sin and gains an eternal life with Him. In worship one finds peace, solace, joy, and comfort. Not having that relationship with God reaps a life of pointless toil, disaffection, emptiness, and ultimately eternal punishment.

Now, these may be very good reasons to *want* to worship God, but these cannot be reasons for *genuine* worship. Recall the example above about the comedian, but let's change a detail. Let's say that the comedian is your friend, and he does not demand that you find his jokes funny but only expresses the sincere hope that you will. Let's also say that you know that if you were to find his jokes funny, your friendship would deepen in very desirable ways, and other benefits to you both would follow. So you really want to find his jokes funny. Alas, this is not sufficient for *actually* finding them funny. Again, you cannot be forced into finding a joke funny, not even by yourself! You can, of course, *say* that you found the jokes funny, and you can even force yourself to laugh at them. But you cannot force yourself to have the genuine attitude of finding them funny. Whether you find the jokes funny is a matter that is largely out of your control. It has to do with the quality of the jokes.

Take a different case. We generally want to like our neighbors. Liking one's neighbors makes the time one spends at home more pleasant, and many other important benefits follow from liking them. But one cannot like one's neighbors on the basis of *that*. There has to be something about *them*—the neighbors themselves—that makes one like them. Genuinely liking the neighbors cannot be based on a calculation of what benefits one can secure by means of liking them. Again, whether you like the neighbors is largely out of your control.

The same goes in the case of worship. One cannot genuinely worship God on the basis of a calculation regarding the benefits of worshipping. You can't *worship* God because it pays. To employ a philosophical term, the benefits of worship are an essential by-product of worship. In other words, when it comes to worship, you can't get what's in it for you if you do it for what's in it for you.

Thus far we have argued that none of the properties regularly associated with God provide a reason why we must worship Him. We think that two important conclusions follow. First, we don't have an obligation to worship God. Second, we shouldn't worship God. As we cannot point to some property that God embodies that makes Him deserving of worship, it is irresponsible to worship God. We are not obligated to worship Him. Furthermore, we have shown that worship requires us to submit our rational capacities to another; this, in turn, renders us incapable of exercising moral agency. But it is by our powers of our moral agency that we are capable of doing good and avoiding evil. In worshipping God, then, we divest ourselves of those capacities by which we can be morally good. And for a rational moral agent to divest himself or herself of these capacities is surely a moral wrong. Therefore, it is wrong to worship God. Indeed, it is wrong for a rational moral creature to worship anything. Accordingly, we are obliged not to worship any entity. And consequently, there is no proper object of worship. And since there is no proper object of worship, God does not exist.

VI. DEFENSES OF WORSHIP

Although we find the argument we just sketched compelling and believe it to be sound, we do not claim to have presented it in all the detail and precision that would be required for it to count as a proof against God's existence. There is still much to be worked out if the problem of worship is to rise to that level. We want in this section to discuss some ways in which a religious believer might respond to the problem of worship. There are several points in the argument in which the religious believer can press competent criticisms.

First of all, the concept of worship is central to the argument and surely deserves further scrutiny. Does worship require obedience? If it requires obedience, does it require *complete* obedience? In presenting our argument, we have supposed that both of these questions should be answered in the affirmative. But we may be wrong. Worship may be best understood as purely expressive and nothing more. That is, one may hold that in worship one *communes with* rather than *takes orders from* God.

This seems a promising avenue for the religious believer to explore. Yet it does render the status of God's commands and one's obligation to God questionable, and we suspect that this would be an unwelcome implication of the proposed defense. Moreover, the idea that worship is simply the expression of one's devotion to God renders the requirement that one worship only *one* God puzzling. If worship is merely the expression of supreme love and devotion, what's so wrong about having those attitudes toward idols, too? It seems to us that worship must have what might be called a *service element*, if the command to worship only one thing is to make sense. But if worship is understood to involve more than the expression of one's devotion, the problem of worship reemerges.

Alternately, a religious believer might contend that worshipping God does not require complete obedience; worshipping God is consistent with sometimes objecting to Him and questioning Him. An interesting story in the Babylonian Talmud is worth recounting here. A group of rabbis is locked in a dispute concerning the appropriate interpretation of divine law. One rabbi, arguing for the minority position, calls out to God to resolve their disagreement. God arrives and declares that the minority opinion is correct, to which the other rabbis, unimpressed, respond that the Torah is "not in heaven" and thus can only be interpreted by humans. Upon hearing of their reaction, God exclaims approvingly, "My children have overruled me!"

It may be said that the problem of worship as we have presented it relies on too rigid a conception of the submission that worship involves. One could hold that worshipping God requires that we do not defer to God's judgment at all but instead employ our own, even in cases in which our judgment seems to run counter to that of God's. In response, we suppose it may still be possible to propitiate such an entity with sacrifices and praise, but it does not seem that such acts would be worship, since this entity is no longer determinative of one's life and thus not the most perfect being. If God needs correction, then God is not worthy of the title.

Another response to the problem might contend that our failure to identify any W-properties does not entail that He doesn't have any. Such an argument may run as follows: God is the proper object of worship, so He has W-properties. We don't know what they are, so instead of inferring that He doesn't have them, we should adopt a more modest attitude. Mysticism and negative theology are then brought in.

Moses Maimonides makes precisely this sort of argument in *The Guide for the Perplexed*:

> God, may He be exalted, cannot be apprehended by the intellects, and
> ... none but He Himself can apprehend what He is, and that apprehension of Him consists in the inability to attain the ultimate term in apprehending Him. (1963: 59)

Maimonides argues for this conception of God precisely in order to maintain the requirement of worship. But we don't see how this reply could work. If we can't say why God is worthy of worship beyond just saying He's God, we're not sure how we could genuinely worship God.

Doesn't worship entail that you have an idea of the thing's greatness and why you're worshipping it? If that's right, you can't just say that you worship God because He's God. One must have some sense of what is it about God that entitles Him to worship. Maimonides' response seems to never get off the ground.

We suppose the premise at issue in our argument is the one that states that one has an obligation to worship something if and only if one can determine that it has a specific W-property. From our perspective, this premise is obviously correct because it derives from a background principle of reason sometimes called *evidentialism*: One should proportion one's commitments to the strength of one's reasons. We admit, however, that this principle is hotly contested, especially in discussions of religious belief. Faith and what people are impelled to believe on its basis are often proposed as counterexamples to evidentialism. This is a useful trump card to be played, and a discussion of faith itself will take us beyond the scope of this book. However, we should note that faith in anything else on the basis of no reasons at all is often called *blind faith*. It gets special reverence in religious contexts, but *blind faith* is a term of contempt in politics and interpersonal relationships because its results are regularly disastrous. We tend to think that abandoning evidentialism in the case of religious belief, too, is simply bad policy. But again there's a serious ongoing debate about these matters.

VII. WRAPPING UP

First, we wanted to present some of the standard atheist considerations concerning the problem of evil. We wanted to show that an atheism driven by the problem of evil embraces many of the familiar moral commitments that religious believers endorse. So the difference between atheists and religious believers is not, as commonly supposed, the difference between two alien moral systems. Rather, atheists and religious believers have remarkably similar moral beliefs. The difference is simply about whether there is a God. Once one recognizes that one's belief about God's existence does not determine one's moral commitments, one should see that the difference between religious believers and atheists is not so monumental after all. In fact, one should see that the difference between the average religious believer and an atheist is likely to be no more drastic than the difference between religious believers of different faiths.

We then sought to outline a different moral case for atheism by raising a new problem for theism: the problem of worship. We presented an argument to the effect that worship is degrading to human dignity. Worship requires complete deference to another, and thus undoes our moral agency. In other words, worship, be it of God or anything else, is bad for our minds. And since worship is bad for us, it is immoral for any being to require it of us. Thus, there is no proper object of worship. And this means that there is no God.

We then highlighted some places where our argument concerning worship can be challenged. We take it as a given that there are thoughtful and serious responses to all our arguments. We are not convinced by these responses, of course, but that does not mean that the people who hold those views are craven or stupid. In fact, we believe that those who believe in God are mistaken and are seriously so. Recall the argument we presented from Maimonides. We do not think negative theology or mysticism is a good solution to the problem of worship. In fact, we believe that Maimonides' arguments actually compound the difficulties we have raised. But Maimonides is nevertheless no dummy, and neither are all the other serious thinkers with whom we have wrestled with in this book.

Answering ultimate questions is often tough going, and we're sure that what we've said here isn't the end of the story. But in the same way we think that there are reasonable challenges to our story, we take it that serious religious believers are bound to recognize the force of the challenges we have presented. Isn't the challenge posed by atheism reasonable? Aren't the values we take a stand on ones worth standing up for? To be sure, we atheists may be mistaken about the relative worth of their value, but our mistakes here are not rooted in a deeper moral corruption. We object to worshipping God for the same reasons that everybody rejects arbitrary authority, invasions of privacy, and requirements of intimacy—they do not respect our personal autonomy. We cannot be complete humans under the tyranny of such requirements.

In the next and final chapter, we will take up some broader questions about politics. More specifically, we will examine some questions concerning the role of religious belief in democratic politics.

NOTES

1. Full text of the address: http://www.americanrhetoric.com/speeches/billygraham911memorial.htm.

2. See Daniel Blake, "Hurricane Katrina: Evangelist Billy Graham & Anglican Head Offer Prayers." *Christianity Today*, September 3, 2005. http://www.christiantoday.com/article/hurricane.katrina.evangelist.billy.graham.anglican.head.offer.prayers/3851.htm.

3. It is worth noting that Pope Benedict recently used this argument during his visit to Auschwitz. He claimed that a world in which God always intervened to prevent cruelty and violence would be a world without freedom. See Jeff Jacoby, "The Silence of God," *Boston Globe*, June 4, 2006.

4. See, for example, the requirement that the righteous rejoice in the punishment that God doles out to those who deserve it (Isaiah 58:10–11).

5. See Tim Bayne and Yujin Nagasawa, "The Grounds of Worship," *Religious Studies* 42 (2006), for an interesting discussion.

CHAPTER SIX

RELIGION IN POLITICS

We hope to have at this point made a powerful case for the reasonableness of atheism. We do not expect to have convinced many readers of the *truth* of atheism. But, to repeat once again, that was not our objective. We aimed rather to demonstrate that atheism is a reasonable position, regardless of whether one holds it to be true. Its reasonableness consists in the fact that atheism is a *rationally defensible* position; it is a position for which compelling reasons can be offered in support and from which one can develop compelling challenges to rival doctrines. In other words, atheism is reasonable in that it can hold its own in the ongoing debates about metaphysics and morality among various stripes of religious believers. But we have shown atheism to be reasonable in another sense as well. We have argued that atheism is consistent with the full range of moral commitments that people often claim lie at the core of their religious convictions. We have argued that atheists can recognize the dignity and inviolability of life, take seriously their moral obligations to others, hold that the world contains objective goods and evils, and can acknowledge the importance of standing up for, and even fighting for, core values such as equality and justice. In fact, we have argued that many adopt atheism for the sake of honoring and upholding those crucial values.

According to the view we have presented in this book, atheism is required by morality. It is the right response for those who seek to take good and evil seriously. It is the proper view for those who want most of all to do the right thing.

One upshot of our argument will no doubt come as a surprise to many. Religion does not have a monopoly on morality and is not the only source of moral insight. In fact, we have presented reasons for thinking that religion can often impede moral insight. At the very least, we have shown that the moral lessons offered by religion must piggyback on our independent moral judgment; if people weren't already capable of competently exercising their moral judgment, belief in God couldn't make them good. For the reasons presented in the previous chapters, good and evil cannot be understood in terms of God's commandments, and religion can't be the basis for morality. Yet we nonetheless acknowledge that freedom, responsibility, justice, peace, kindness, generosity, fairness, and equality are all religious values. But this means that they are often recognized and prized by various popular religions. These values are not the sole property of the religious.

Consequently, the common view of atheists as opportunistic, selfish, and irresponsible immoralists must be abandoned. Atheism is consistent with views that recognize objective rights and wrongs, goods and evils. Moreover, there is nothing in religious belief that aids one in grounding moral belief or demonstrating that morality is objective. As Plato saw so clearly, there is no clear way to ground the objectivity of morality on God. More important, neither atheism nor religious belief makes one a good person. Whether one is good depends on one's actions and one's character. Belief in God, or lack thereof, is largely irrelevant.

Once these points are accepted, religious believers can no longer take the difference between themselves and atheists to be a deep *moral* difference. That is, there is no great moral divide between atheists and religious believers. We all value justice and despise cruelty. We seek to instill moral and intellectual virtues in our children. We prize liberty and individual autonomy. We recognize the dignity of other human beings and seek to treat them with respect. We look upon violence and war as bad things that are sadly sometimes necessary. We endeavor to alleviate suffering. We seek peace. To be sure, people disagree in specific cases over what justice requires, how far individual liberty should extend, what it is to respect others, and so on. But these disagreements are not peculiar to atheists and religious believers. Members of different religions sharply disagree over such matters. Indeed, members of the *same* religion disagree about fundamental moral questions. As it turns out, the moral difference between any given atheist and any given religious believer is likely to not be more dramatic than the moral difference between any two religious believers.

The overwhelming majority of Jews, Christians, Muslims, Buddhists, Confucians, Taoists, and others have reconciled themselves to the fact that reasonable people can disagree over religion. They have resolved to coexist in relative peace with those who they are religiously bound to regard as seriously mistaken about God. They often prove themselves capable of showing each other respect, despite the fact that they ultimately disagree over who God is. Most important, they recognize a moral duty to afford to each person the freedom to follow his or her conscience in matters of religious faith. They accordingly stand ready to regard those with whom they disagree over even the most important matters as fellow citizens and political equals.

In light of the arguments we have presented in this book, religious believers should see atheists in roughly the same way that they see persons of different faiths. To the Christian, the atheist should be no more foreign than the Jew. Both the atheist and the Jew deny that Jesus was divine, and that is to deny the definitive claim of Christianity. In fact, Christians and Jews often see each other as seriously mistaken about important religious matters. Yet they generally acknowledge the moral imperative to respect each other. Likewise, religious believers should see atheists as seriously mistaken and perhaps in spiritual peril, but nonetheless reasonable people who are fully equal citizens and thus deserving of respect. In this final chapter, then, we want to articulate a few of the political implications of adopting the view that religious believers and atheists alike are equal citizens and deserving of respect.

I. THE MORAL CORE OF MODERN DEMOCRACY

Our discussion of these matters begins with a quick sketch of some ideas that are likely to strike our readers as quite familiar. Modern democracy, the form of democracy practiced today in the United States and throughout much of the Western world, differs from ancient democracy in several respects. One such respect is perhaps most important of all. Modern democracy is *constitutional* democracy. Consider the contrast. Ancient democracies were based in the simple principle of majority rule. When a question arose that needed a decision, people were asked to vote, and the majority view ruled. Modern democracy does indeed employ the principle of majority rule, but there are officially acknowledged constraints placed on what decisions majorities can make. In a constitutional democracy, for example, you cannot be voted into slavery. No matter how many people want you to be enslaved, you are a free person. This is because there is a constitution that specifies certain measures that majorities, even overwhelming majorities, cannot take.

In the United States, many of these constraints are specified in the Bill of Rights, the first ten amendments to the US Constitution. For example, in the First Amendment, it is famously specified that the government cannot infringe on freedom of religion, speech, the press, assembly, and petition. What this means, among other things, is that each individual has the right to speak his or her mind, even if an over-whelming majority of people would rather that he or she didn't. The constitution provides protection to the individual from the will of the majority. It affirms that there are certain things that even a vast majority cannot impose on even a minority of one. Ancient democracy makes no such provision for individual liberty.

The focus on individual liberty in constitutional democracy is important because it manifests a general attitude—often associated with British philosopher John Locke and clearly adopted by Thomas Jefferson and other founders of the United States—that governments exist to *serve* their people. Note the contrast with monarchy. Where there's a king, the people are his subjects; the people serve the king. In a constitutional democracy, however, the government serves the people. In fact, in a constitutional democracy, the government *is* the people.

The philosophical commitment underlying the view that government exists for the sake of serving the people it governs may now seem commonplace, but in fact it is nothing short of revolutionary. Governments are created by people for specific purposes; they accordingly exist for the sake of achieving those purposes. In the days of kingdoms, it was thought that governments existed by divine right. There were kings, and they deserved to rule because God chose them to rule. The view associated with Locke and Jefferson explicitly denies this. The government serves the people, and there are governments because the people choose to create them. This implies that humans are born into complete freedom, with no master and no rulers, and come to be subject to civil and social rules only by their own choosing.

Now for the revolutionary part. If governments exist because the people choose for there to be a government, and if governments thus exist for the purpose of serving the people who have chosen to create them, then the people are at liberty to overthrow their government if it proves unable or unwilling to serve its appointed purpose. In the Declaration of Independence, Jefferson could not be more forceful on this point. He writes:

> Prudence, indeed, will dictate that Governments long established should not be changed for light and transient causes; and accordingly all experience hath shewn that mankind are more disposed to suffer, while evils are sufferable than to right themselves by abolishing the forms to which they are accustomed. But when a long train of abuses and usurpations, pursuing invariably the same Object evinces a design to reduce them under absolute Despotism, it is their right, it is their duty, to throw off such Government, and to provide new Guards for their future security.

Jefferson's message is clear. When a government proves unable to serve its people and instead seeks to make its people its subjects, then not only is it permitted that the people overthrow their government, it is their *duty* to do so. Such is the thought that started the Revolutionary War in North America. This is potent, breathtaking stuff. And it was virtually unthinkable at the time.

The important thing to note here is that Jefferson's view is driven by several background ideas. One, which has already been mentioned, is the idea that individuals are naturally free, and they come to be under the government's authority only by choosing to do so. In John Locke's *Second Treatise of Government* (1690), this idea is presented as the claim that governments get their authority to rule by the consent of the governed (IV.22). This brings into view a second background idea, namely, that individuals are by nature equal. Since governments gain their authority only by winning the consent of those to be governed, each individual is not only free but also an equal participant in authorizing the government to govern. In other words, no one is subject to the rule of the government because someone else has said so. Every person who is subject to the government's rule must consent. A third but especially important idea behind Jefferson's view is that even once a government is established by consent, that consent can be revoked. The people can undo the government and render it illegitimate. Of course, there are very special conditions under which a government can be rightly revolted against and dissolved. Once we establish a government, we can't just dissolve it willy-nilly; otherwise, criminals would simply have to state that they do not consent to the rule of the government, and they would properly be set free. No. Once established, a government can be dissolved only under special conditions. The text of the US Declaration is mainly devoted to outlining the abuses of the British king; its aim is to justify revolution.

There is a lot to say about these matters. The point worth emphasizing here is that one condition governments must meet if they are to retain their legitimacy is that they must treat each person under its jurisdiction as a free and equal citizen. Of course, this does not mean that governments cannot force citizens to pay taxes, avoid speeding, or refrain from killing others. The government is in the business of forcing people to do what they might not otherwise do. But the government is constrained in this task by the need to treat every citizen as a political equal. This means that the government cannot randomly impose laws on you. Nor can it specifically pick you out and make laws that govern you alone. Again, it must treat all citizens as equals.

Importantly, it must also be able to *justify* to you what it does. Again, when the government imposes a law, it necessarily forces people to do what they might not otherwise do. And when the government forces people to do something, it *coerces* them and impinges on their freedom. So when a government coerces free and equal citizens, it must have a *reason* to do so. And, moreover, that reason must be of the *right kind*. To put the matter bluntly, when a government coerces, it must be able to provide a reason for the coercion that does not violate its commitment to the freedom and equality of every citizen. In other words, a government that rules over free and equal citizens must be *accountable* to them.

An example will help. Imagine that the US government has just passed a law forbidding citizens over the age of eighteen from chewing gum. Suppose that the president holds a press conference reporting the news from Congress that gum chewing is hereby illegal, except for children. This law would be in many respects silly. But one thing that would make it *unjust* is that it is difficult to see how the government could justify this curtailment of liberty. Some people, after all, very much enjoy chewing gum. Why make it illegal? Note that the impulse to question the law is itself an inheritance from Locke and Jefferson. Governments are supposed to do things that *serve* us; they do not get to simply push us around or issue orders. When the government imposes a requirement on us, we have the right to ask why. And the government must answer.

So let's say that the president recognizes the need to give a reason in favor of the new law. He or she says that the Congress has declared that adults who chew gum look silly. He or she goes on to say that the government has decided that it's bad to look silly. So chewing gum is not permitted.

Something's gone wrong here. But what? To criticize the law, must we argue that gum chewing in fact *doesn't* make adults look silly? Must we argue that it's not bad to look silly? No. One can accept the claims that chewing gum makes adults look silly and that it's bad to look silly yet object to the law. This is because the problem with the law is that the proposed justification for it presents a reason of the wrong kind. In short, governments are not supposed to act to ensure that some citizens do not look silly. For better or worse, part of what it means to treat citizens as free and equal is to allow them to do things that might make them look silly. Citizens are free to look silly if they want to. Indeed, they are free to'believe that gum chewing doesn't make them look silly at all. Or they are free to not care in the least about whether they look silly.

Consider a contrasting case. As we all know, the government does not allow citizens to drive their cars while intoxicated. Drunk driving is a crime. In fact, it's rightfully treated as a very serious offense. Why? How does the prohibition on drunk driving differ from the prohibition on gum chewing? Why not say that people should be free to decide when to drive their cars? Some people enjoy taking risks with their lives. They should be free to live as they wish. Why does the government get to say that they cannot drive drunk?

Here's the reason. Drunk drivers place others at significant risk of harm and injury. It is the government's job to protect its citizens, to also protect them from injury, and to keep them from injuring each other. People are certainly at liberty to decide whether to drink to excess. They are free to incur the health risks associated with excessive drinking. But they are not free to place *others* at risk. So the government makes it illegal to drive drunk. And it has a reason of the right kind for doing so, a reason that is consistent with treating all citizens as free and equal.

Thus far, we have said that a distinctive feature of modern constitutional democracy is the commitment to the freedom and equality of all citizens. When it comes to coercive government action, this commitment plays out in the idea that a government must be able to justify itself to its citizens. There is a burden on the government to say why it acts as it does. And the justification must be of the right kind. Specifically, governmental justification for coercion must employ reasons that are consistent with treating every citizen as free and equal. This commitment to regarding each person as a free and equal citizen is the moral core of modern democracy.

II. GOVERNMENT NEUTRALITY

The image we have just sketched of modern democracy is in several respects incomplete. We cannot hope to elaborate on all the important aspects of democracy in this chapter. But there's one loose end that needs attention. We asserted that the government must act in ways that are consistent with treating each citizen as free and equal. We then sketched two easy cases, one in which a law was proposed and could not be justified in the right way and another involving an easily justified law. But examples go only so far toward an explanation. What is the difference between a law designed to save adults from silliness and a law designed to protect citizens from injury? What is it about the latter case that it is consistent with the requirement that the government must treat each citizen as free and equal? What is it about the former case that makes the proposed justification a failure? Obviously, we need to say more.

One of the central freedoms recognized by modern democracy is what we might call *intellectual freedom*. To respect the freedom and equality of its citizens, governments must recognize the capacity of individuals to form, revise, examine, challenge, and defend ideas. Citizens must be free to decide for themselves what makes a life good, what values are most important, what is worth pursuing, and in short how to live. They must be granted *freedom of conscience*, the freedom to live in accordance with their own best judgment concerning questions about how to live. The recognition of intellectual freedom is what drives many of the fundamental rights specified in the Bill of Rights. But note that individual freedom to live in accordance with one's convictions is not unconstrained. One who sincerely believes that the good life consists of hunting and murdering other people cannot live according to his or her convictions. Neither can the drunk driver who thinks that the thrill of impaired driving is what makes life worth living. The reason is obvious: one's freedom is constrained by the freedom of others. One is free to live according to one's convictions about how to live only up to a point; one cannot infringe on others' liberty to live as one sees fit. Some views about how to live are impermissible in a society of free and equal citizens. To put the point in a familiar way, each of us is free to live as we wish so long as we do not infringe on the rights of others to live as they themselves see fit.

What this means is that in living our own lives we, like our government, must recognize and respect the freedom and equality of our fellow citizens. We are not permitted to put them at risk for the sake of pursuing our own sense of the good life. We are required to recognize that others have their own sense of how best to live, and if that vision of the good life falls within the bounds of permissibility, we must afford others the space to pursue their own vision of the good life, even if we think they are seriously mistaken.

Consider another example. There is no doubt that some of our readers sincerely believe that atheists are in serious moral and spiritual danger. In their view, atheists have imperiled their immortal souls and thus are making a tragic mistake, one that they will regret for eternity. Someone who sincerely believes this will of course feel the need to morally rescue atheists. Perhaps this rescue will take the form of trying to convince atheists that they are in error. Maybe it will consist in giving to the atheist a copy of the Bible and urging him or her to read it. Maybe the rescue attempt will involve warning the atheist of what happens to those in hell and praying to God for assistance in changing the atheist's mind. We, the authors, have been subject to these measures, and, though they are annoying, we put up with these attempts to save our souls. We say they are annoying, but there is another sense in which they are touching. Every time someone is willing to come to our house and knock on our door to discuss the prospects of salvation with us, we are also genuinely appreciative—someone has gone out of his or her way to share with us very important information. We think this information is also very much in error, but insofar as these people knocking on our doors on Saturday mornings think it is true, it is an act of kindness to ensure that those who have not heard the Good News hear it. We repay this kindness with a cup of coffee and some argument.

But now imagine someone taking a different kind of measure with atheists. Consider, as before, a religious believer who sincerely believes that atheists are in serious moral peril and thus in need of spiritual rescue. But imagine that the believer in question employs the following strategy: she kidnaps atheists, drugs them, and while they are unconscious, baptizes them. Or, alternatively, consider a religious believer who forces atheists to attend church services at gunpoint.

We think it is clear that taking such measures is not only illegal but immoral. One simply *cannot* treat a fellow citizen in that way and claim to be committed to treating others are free and equal. In kidnapping atheists or forcing them to participate in religion in some other way, one adopts the stance of being the atheist's *custodian* or tutor. One takes oneself to be superior to the atheist, and thus fit to direct his life, even against his will. This attitude is inconsistent with regarding the atheist as a fellow citizen, a free and equal person.

A similar point holds in the case of government. The government fails to treat its citizens as free and equal when it coerces them in the service of some specific vision of the good life. Imagine a government that required its citizens to attend services at the local temple. Imagine the government declaring that it has been determined that Judaism is the true religion and thus is correct about how people should live. Such a law would raise some of the same concerns evoked by the chewing-gum law discussed earlier. One needn't renounce Judaism to find the law objectionable. One could indeed accept Judaism but still find the law in question unjust. Why? Because governments are not in the business of deciding for their citizens the question of which religion is correct. Nor are they in the business of deciding for their citizens the question of how to live a good life. They are instead in the business of creating and maintaining social order in a way that respects the freedom and equality of all citizens. And this requires governments to keep their nose out of life's Big Questions and leave it to the citizens themselves to work out their own views about how to live.

This is to say that governments must be *neutral* when it comes to questions concerning the good life and how individuals should live. To be clear, government neutrality does *not* mean that the government must regard the life of the philanthropist and the life of the serial murderer as equally good. The requirement to be neutral is not a call for relativism or non-judgmentalism. The state opposes the way of life of the serial murderer because it does not respect the freedom and equality of all. That is, the state can recognize and act on the basis of *moral commitments*. Indeed, it is required to respect the freedom and equality of its citizens. What the state cannot do is deliberately take sides in moral disputes among those visions of the good life that are consistent with treating everyone as free and equal. Among those visions of the good life that are permissible in a constitutional democracy, the government must be neutral.

This means that the government cannot enact laws on the basis of, say, papal declarations. For example, were the government to enact a law declaring it illegal to eat meat on Fridays during Lent, it would be violating the moral requirement of treating all citizens as free and equal. This is because citizens are free to reject the authority of the pope and, too, all Catholic teachings. They are free to reject Catholicism precisely because it is possible to reject Catholicism and yet remain committed to treating others as free and equal. A law forcing all citizens to follow Catholic teachings would therefore be analogous to kidnapping atheists and forcing them to be baptized. And this is unjust.

To treat citizens as free and equal, governments must adopt a stance of neutrality among the various conceptions of the good life—religious and secular—that citizens are at liberty to accept. Just as a modern democratic government cannot rightly enact a law forbidding gum-chewing, it cannot enact a law requiring religious observance. Just as a modern democratic government cannot enact a law on the basis of its judgment about what makes adults look silly, it cannot enact a law on the basis of its judgment about what makes souls pure. It is not the job of government to save citizens' souls any more than it is its job to prevent citizens from looking silly. To offer such reasons in justification of a law is to offer a reason of the wrong kind, and thus to fail at the task of justifying the law to those who are subject to it. To put the point otherwise, when the government enacts laws, it must be able to provide its citizens with reasons that they *all* can recognize, no matter what their individual conceptions of the good life may be.

III. THE ETHICS OF CITIZENSHIP

We have already noted that in a constitutional democracy, the government *is* the people. In the previous section, we argued that a constitutional democracy must be neutral among permissible conceptions of the good. We specified that this means when the government enacts a law, it must be able to justify it with reasons that all citizens could recognize.

To get a better grasp of this requirement, consider a law banning smoking in enclosed public places. Were the government to offer as a justification of this law the reason that, say, smoking is unbecoming, it would fail to meet its burden of justifying the law. Similarly, were the government to offer as a reason for the law the claim that The Bible forbids public smoking (assume that the Bible indeed forbids it), it would also fail to justify the law. It would fail to justify the law, too, if it offered the explanation that smoking is unhealthy for the smokers. The reason is clear: free and equal citizens are at liberty to engage in unbecoming behavior, they are at liberty to reject the Bible's teachings, and they may elect to take certain kinds of health risks. These are all reasons of the wrong kind.

But now consider a different justification. The government bans smoking in enclosed public places because it has sufficient evidence that secondhand smoke poses a significant health risk to nonsmokers. In banning smoking in enclosed public places, the government indeed curtails the liberty of those who choose to smoke. But it does so for the sake of protecting those who choose not to smoke from significant risks. It is for the sake of protecting the freedom and equality of all that the government curtails the freedom of those who choose to engage in an activity that is potentially harmful to others. Protecting others who choose to not take certain risks with their health is a reason of the right kind, one that can be recognized by anyone committed to the idea that citizens must be treated as free and equal. The ban on smoking in enclosed public places is therefore justified.

Now let's raise a difficulty. Again, in a constitutional democracy, the government is the people. This means that the government is *accountable* to the people it serves. It also means that many government roles and offices are filled by popular elections. We vote for officials, officeholders, and representatives. Those holding these positions are charged with conducting the business of government on our behalf. To be sure, sometimes citizens are called upon to vote directly on some question of public policy. But for the most part, when we elect people to serve in government, we authorize them to make decisions in our stead and in our name. They govern so that we can pursue other things in life. In short, in a democracy, government is accountable to us but this means that we are *responsible* for it. There is a government because we *make* it; we *authorize* a government by means of our actions as citizens. Accordingly, citizenship involves actions that can be performed well or badly, responsibly or carelessly, and so on. There is therefore an ethics of citizenship.

And here's the puzzle. If government cannot enact laws on the basis of reasons of the wrong kind, is it wrong for citizens to decide how to vote by appealing to that kind of reason? It would be wrong for the government to enact a law on the basis of some pronouncement by the pope; does this entail that it would be wrong for a citizen to decide whom to vote for by appealing to papal decrees? Let's look at an example. Let's say that the pope, or some other religious figure taken by large numbers of religious believers to be authoritative, declares that stem cells are instances of sacred human life and thus must not be used in experiments. It would be wrong for the government to ban experiments using stem cells on the grounds that the pope (or some other religious official) has forbidden such experiments. That the pope has said something does not by itself provide a reason for the government to act, since free and equal citizens are at liberty to regard the pope as nothing more than an obscenely wealthy crackpot in a funny costume.

Next, let us stipulate what might very well be true, namely, that there is no reason to morally oppose stem cell experimentation that does not employ the concept of sacredness. If we wanted to speak loosely, we could say that we are stipulating that there is no moral reason to oppose stem cell experimentation that is not intrinsically religious in nature. But let's try to be a little more precise: there is no moral reason against stem cell experimentation that does not employ moral concepts that free and equal citizens are at liberty to reject. If this stipulation is granted, it is clear that there is no reason of the right kind for the government of a constitutional democracy to prohibit stem cell experimentation. Any prohibition would be unjustifiable.

But consider the matter from the point of view of Sally, a Catholic citizen. For Sally, the papal pronouncement on the ethics of stem cell experimentation counts as a decisive piece of moral instruction. Since the pope has forbidden stem cell experimentation, Sally must regard it as a serious moral wrong, a violation of human life. Accordingly, Sally must regard a government policy permitting stem cell experimentation as a serious injustice. As she wants to avoid complicity in injustice, she decides to vote only for candidates who have publicly expressed their moral opposition to stem cell experimentation and have promised to work to enact legislation to prohibit it. So, on Election Day, Sally votes only for candidates who oppose stem cell experimentation. Has Sally acted wrongly?

Now let's be clear that we are not asking whether Sally has committed a crime. We are not considering a view according to which voting on the basis of one's religious convictions is criminal. But we are raising a puzzle about constitutional democracy. More specifically, we are raising a question about the morality of citizenship. Again, it would be wrong for the government to ban stem cell experiments, because the only reasons that can be offered are of the wrong kind. Does it follow that it's wrong for Sally to wield her share of political power on behalf of a ban on stem cell experimentation? Or, to put the matter more directly, if it would be wrong for the government to pass a law, is it therefore wrong for citizens to vote in ways that would compel government to pass that law?

We think that the answer to this question is yes. Citizens should refrain from voting on the sole basis of their religious convictions. We hold that this position follows from the more general position we articulated above regarding the appropriate bases of government action. To repeat, when government enacts laws, it coerces its citizens. For that coercion to be consistent with the requirement that governments treat their citizens as free and equal, the government must justify what it does to its citizens. And again this means that the government must be able to offer its citizens reasons for the coercion that the citizens can recognize as reasons. This means that reasons of a sectarian nature—reasons that draw their force from some religious perspective, for instance—are not reasons of the right kind. Such reasons do not accomplish the justificatory task.

Now, it seems clear to us that if it would be wrong for the government to do something, it would be wrong to tell the government to do it. And votes are the instruments by which citizens tell the government what to do. So if it would be wrong for the government to enact a ban on stem cell experimentation, it's wrong for Sally to cast her votes solely for the sake of instructing the government to enact such a law. She is, in effect, attempting to get the government to act in a way that treats some of her fellow citizens as less than free and equal. She thereby has violated her duties of citizenship. Sally's wrongdoing of course is not criminal. We are not proposing that Sally should be punished. Our claim is simply that Sally has acted in a way that runs counter to how a citizen should act. Her action, though not criminal, is at the very least not admirable.

IV. THE FREE EXERCISE OF RELIGION

We expect that our view of the ethics of citizenship will raise the hackles of many religious believers. Many will contend that it is part of the *free exercise* of their religion that they act as a citizen in ways that are informed by their religious convictions. They will contend that part of what it is to be, say, a Christian is to look to the moral teachings of the Bible in deciding how to act as a citizen. They will argue that it is a *religious obligation* to do so; to require citizens to abandon their religious obligations when acting as a citizen is unjust. In fact, some may go further and contend that the ethics of citizenship we have proposed proves how disingenuous we, the authors, have been throughout this entire book; we have proven ourselves to be uninterested in respectful debate, and instead we seek to silence religious believers.

This is a serious set of charges. And it is a popular line of response, too. We often hear arguments to the effect that religious belief is under attack in the United States and that the sinister forces of secularism are being mobilized to sweep the public square clean of religious belief. The yearly "War on Christmas" in the United States is just one manifestation of the concern. But before things get too heated, allow us to clarify a few elements of the ethics of citizenship we have proposed. We think that the view we have proposed is not subject to the usual criticisms. Moreover, we think that religious believers themselves have good reason to adopt our view of the ethics of citizenship.

First of all, nothing we have proposed aims to prohibit *speech*. We have not argued that Sally should be forbidden from speaking in religious language against the moral permissibility of stem cell experimentation. She is of course free to speak her mind. She is of course free to try to convince her fellow citizens, including those citizens who are scientists, that such experiments are morally impermissible. She can form or join activist groups that aspire to raise awareness of the moral impropriety of stem cell experimentation. She can write letters to her representatives expressing her views. She can publish and distribute pamphlets, editorials, and essays presenting her case. And she can, within the specified legal parameters, protest, agitate, picket, and demonstrate on behalf of her views. In short, the ethics of citizenship we have described applies only to certain specific acts of citizenship, namely, those designed to directly instruct the government to enact a coercive law.

Picking up on this last point, we want to emphasize, second, that the ethics of citizenship we have proposed does not apply to *all* acts of government. Governments sometimes act in ways that coerce no one. They declare that certain days are holidays, for example. We have no objection to the government recognizing December 25 as Christmas Day. More important, we also recognize that there are some cases where government must make policy decisions in which it would be impossible or inadvisable to not appeal to intrinsically religious reasons. In deciding where to allow developers to build a new shopping mall, it might be fully appropriate to consider the relative locations of local churches and cemeteries. The ethics of belief we endorse is concerned to place moral constraints on the reasons citizens employ when nontrivial matters are at stake. Of course, there will be room for disagreement about when a given matter is nontrivial. But there are some clear cases. The government's policy on stem cell experiments will very likely determine whether scientists will soon find cures for certain debilitating diseases; the lives and well-being of many who are ill are implicated in the stem cell debate.

Third, in our example above, we were careful to stipulate that no nonreligious reason was available to support the ban on stem cell experimentation. But in most real-world cases, this stipulation does not hold. That is, most often there are reasons that can be raised in favor of (or against) a policy proposal. Consider a proposed legal ban on certain interrogation techniques that seem to cross the line into torture. Perhaps Sally supports such a ban on the basis of her religious convictions concerning the sacredness of human life. But surely there are other reasons that may be produced in favor of the ban. One could oppose torture on the basis of the dignity of human beings, or the importance of acting in ways that do not violate human rights, and so on. Our ethics of citizenship does not require Sally to *discount* or *deny* her religious reason for supporting the ban on torture. She may vote on the basis of her religious reasons in ways designed to compel the government to adopt the ban. That she is motivated by her religious reasons does not matter because the policy she endorses also enjoys the support of reasons of the right kind. To put the point differently, our ethics of citizenship requires Sally to refrain from voting for a policy that can be supported *only* by her religious reasons. In cases in which her religious reasons favor a policy that is supported by reasons of the right kind, Sally does no wrong in voting on the basis of her religious reasons.

Fourth, it should be noted that the ethics of citizenship we have proposed implies no definite position concerning the moral permissibility of there being *religious exemptions* from standing laws and policies. The question of whether a religious reason could ever suffice to justify an exemption from a law is different from the question of whether a religious reason is ever sufficient to justify a law. There are many familiar cases involving legal accommodations for members of certain religious sects that are without a doubt fascinating and morally important. We can take no view here on questions of whether, for example, the Amish should be exempt from certain forms of taxation, or Sikhs should be exempt from laws requiring motorcyclists to wear helmets. Religious reasons might be an adequate basis for accommodation, but maybe not. Our view is focused on a different question.

Finally, we are willing to acknowledge that there are legitimate and sincere conflicts of conscience, cases in which citizens are tragically torn between their religious convictions and civic obligations. We are willing to allow that in crucial cases involving life and death and other momentous matters, religious believers can find themselves truly divided, even tortured. But we note that the conflict between religious conviction and civic obligation is possible only when one recognizes that one's civic obligations are different from the requirements that derive from one's religious beliefs. In such cases, we can understand why religious citizens might resolve to act on the basis of their religious conviction alone. Again, we think that such a citizen does wrong. But we nonetheless can appreciate the difficulty of having to deal with conflicting obligations and realize that sometimes citizens have compelling excuses for falling short of their civic obligations.

Now, it seems to us that once these clarifications are in place, we can dismiss the charge that our ethics of citizenship constitutes a violation of religious citizens' rights to free exercise. Again, the issue is not about the free exercise of one's religion. The question is whether it could be right to try to use the power of the government to force others to live in accordance with one's own religious convictions. Free exercise does not afford this right to religious believers. So our ethics of citizenship does not run afoul of free exercise.

V. WHY RELIGIOUS BELIEVERS SHOULD ACCEPT OUR VIEW

Perhaps the foregoing arguments suffice to show that the ethics of citizenship we have proposed does not violate anyone's right to free exercise of religion. But the ethics of citizenship might still be the source of unease among religious believers. They may be wary of any attempt to constrain the public and political role their religious convictions can play. We think this is a likely reaction to what we have proposed. So we want to give religious believers a positive argument for adopting our suggested ethics of citizenship.

The idea that citizens may not base their voting behavior solely on their religious conviction may seem dubious when we consider the matter from the perspective of competing religious and nonreligious reasons for public policy. But the matter takes on a decidedly different hue when considered from the point of view of the reasons provided by competing religious faiths.

So let's consider Stan. Stan is a local Satanist. His religious convictions require him to attempt to get the government to enact a law calling for government-sanctioned hedonism festivals involving public orgies, blood rituals, alcohol consumption, and animal sacrifice. To avoid difficulties, let's say that the festival involves no compulsory acts of worship and no forced interpersonal contact. Stan's hedonism festivals are more like state-sanctioned public fraternity parties than compulsory church attendance. Stan supports this law on the basis of his strictly Satanic reasons, and there are no other reasons to support the law he favors. So Stan engages in activities of citizenship designed to compel the government to enact his favored law.

Of course, Stan is unlikely to succeed politically. However, notice that if we reject an ethics of citizenship that places constraints on what can count as a reason of the right kind for governmental action, we confront an implication that should be worrisome to many religious believers. If the ethics of citizenship that we have proposed is rejected, then non-Satanist religious citizens are required to recognize the *in principle* legitimacy of a law that enjoys no other justification than Stan's Satanic one. In other words, when the ethics of citizenship that we have proposed is rejected, Christian, Jewish, Muslim, and Buddhist citizens place themselves under political conditions that would morally permit coercion on the basis of reasons that they not only do not recognize the moral force of, but are religiously committed to *denying* the moral force of. In rejecting the ethics of citizenship, religious citizens make themselves vulnerable to justified coercion on the basis of reasons they, from their religious perspectives, must deny are reasons at all.

So let's imagine that Stan somehow prevails. If the ethics of citizenship is rejected, the Christian citizen has no principled objection to Stan's law. More important, if Stan prevails, Christian citizens would have a moral obligation to do what they are religiously obliged to deny they could ever have a *moral* reason to do, namely, recognize the legitimacy of a government that enacts laws on the sole basis of Satanic reasons. We must confess that this seems untenable, bordering on incoherent.

Perhaps the case of Stan seems too farfetched. Let's consider a different example. Marco is a Marx-inspired Christian Liberation Theologian. One element of Marco's religion is the belief that violent conflict is inevitable in the pursuit of justice. Accordingly, Marco sees the compulsory conscription into military combat forces as a necessary solidarity-building and conscience-purifying measure. In fact, Marco holds, again on the basis of his religion, that children should be exposed to military discipline as soon as they are able, and he thinks that children are ready for conscription at twelve years old. Now, Marco is religiously obligated to act as a citizen in ways that would promote legislation requiring the conscription into military combat forces of twelve-year-olds. He has no other reasons than his religious ones for promoting this law; indeed, no other reason exists. But he nonetheless acts as a citizen on the basis of his religious reasons for the law he favors.

Let's suppose that Marco prevails. Where does that leave citizens who reject Marco's religious beliefs, including those religious citizens who are religiously obligated to endorse pacifism? The religious pacifists who are Marco's fellow citizens must now see themselves as under a moral obligation to participate in combat, despite the fact that they must also regard combat as generally impermissible.

It seems, then, religious believers ought to support our ethics of citizenship. They ought to admit that citizens devoted to the ideas of freedom and equality owe to each other a special regard and respect that requires them to avoid trying to employ the coercive power of the government on behalf of some policy or law that can be supported only from their own set of religious beliefs. They ought to agree that when one favors a law that can be supported only by the reasons provided by one's own particular religious view, one generally ought to refrain from supporting it. When we act as citizens, we must act as equal partners in a common civic project, despite deep religious differences. When we act as citizens, that is, we must act on the basis of our best judgment about what treating *all* citizens as free and equal requires. Other, more ambitious, moral goals lie outside the purview of politics. And that's a testament to the importance of those broader moral concerns.

We imagine that our argument will be met with the following response from some religious believers: Stan the Satanist and Marco the Marxist would never win their cases here in the United States, as the vast majority of Americans are Christians. Views like Stan's and Marco's would never win many votes in an election; they would never win enough votes to win a ballot initiative. Thus, we don't have to worry about folks like this getting electoral support, because traditional Christians won't vote for these policies.

There are two problems with this response. First, the response presumes that traditional Christian commitments are the norm in most US communities, but this is no longer a reliable presumption. There are large Jewish and Muslim voting blocs in many parts of the United States, and Eastern religions are quickly gaining in many precincts. The presumption that non-Christian viewpoints would never win popular support in elections is becoming weaker and weaker as the demographics change. So it is a shortsighted policy to put religion at the core of political judgment.

The second problem is one of principle. The response to our argument concerning the ethics of citizenship is that people of religion X or Y are in the minority and so must submit to the religious dictates of those in the majority. But here is the problem. This attitude marks a failure to appreciate the conscience and freedom of people who hold minority religious views. Is being in the minority a reason to be treated as a second-class citizen? Imagine that Montana became a state that recognized the divinity of only Ra the Egyptian Sun God. All state employees were to take Ra's birthday off and do a special dance and sacrifice for the summer solstice. Imagine you lived in Montana, and your children were required to take part in a special blood sacrifice every morning for Ra in the public schools. Imagine that your neighbors and employers resented your resistance to these rules. "Why do you have to be so difficult?" they would ask. "This is the way we do it here," they would remind you. "If you don't like it here, then you should leave." But suppose that you like Montana. Suppose that you find Montana beautiful and the people wonderful (except for the religious oppression). Yet your neighbors look at you not as an equal but as an outlier that must be brought into line, silenced, and converted. And they use state power to bring that about. This is oppression. And this is precisely what it is to be in the religious minority in the United States—to be overtly reminded that you are a minority, to be ignored in most policy discussions of religion for the only reason that your commitments are not those of the majority, and to be treated as someone whose view on religious matters is not relevant.

We presume that you are committed to the core commitments of the modern democratic project, namely, that the government's legitimacy depends on the consent of *all* the governed. If so, then the majoritarian sentiment behind the objection that neither Stan nor Marco could ever have a chance of winning is beside the point. So long as you regard oppression of a minority as acceptable, you've given up the very project of modern constitutional democracy, the kind that protects the rights of individuals. Protecting the rights of individuals is about protecting the conscience of minorities, even if they may be irritating and perhaps rude. Yes, neither Stan the Satanist nor Marco the Marxist will win any ballot initiative. But that fact is irrelevant in the case we are considering; we are examining the issue of how governments and societies can respect the rights of individuals, even those who may be in a tiny minority. We have been proposing situations in which you can imagine yourself as a member of a religious minority or in which a vocal minority you reject wins a crucial political victory. Once you imagine yourself in such a situation, you can see what it is like to have no political recourse to protect your life and what you sincerely believe is correct. When a government can force you to act in violation of your conscience, it's hard to say that you're free at all.

The solution is not to bring politics into line with one's religious convictions. The solution rather is to secularize politics. It is crucial to note that secularized politics does not amount to politics in the service of a secular worldview. The aim instead is to practice democracy in ways that fully acknowledge and respect the fact that on matters of religion, there is room for reasonable disagreement among free and equal citizens. A secularized politics attempts to respect religious difference by refusing to govern on the basis of any particular religious doctrine. In short, secularism is not the attempt to eradicate religion or erase it from society, but to respect it.

VI. IN CONCLUSION

In this book, we have sought to start an argument. We have sought to convince religious believers not that their religious beliefs are false and atheism is true, but rather that their beliefs *about* atheism are false. We have tried to show that atheists can produce powerful criticisms of most common forms of religious belief while also providing compelling accounts of morality and democratic politics. We have tried to show that atheists can take religious belief seriously and yet reject God's existence.

We have tried, too, to show that rejecting God's existence does not require us to shy away from serious moral conviction.

We have also tried to set the stage for an ongoing argument between religious believers and atheists. We have tried to lay the groundwork for a civil and reasonable public debate about God, morality, and democracy. With this aim in mind, we have tried to articulate a workable conception of responsible, intellectual engagement among adversaries. Indeed, in these pages, we have tried to put this conception into practice.

THE PROBLEM OF HELL

✣

Hell, we are told, is a place of everlasting torment. That torment has been described in a number of ways: a lake of fire, a pit of darkness, a burning wind. Jesus described hell as a place where the damned are burned by an "unquenchable fire" (Mark 9:42). There have been other imagined torments, usually including being tortured at the hands of demons or Satan himself. Dante envisioned demons flaying the damned, and he described Satan as continually chewing on Brutus, Cassius, and Judas. That hell is a place of torment makes it a bad place, to be sure. What makes it even worse is that in hell the torment is *everlasting*. The fire that burns the damned is *unquenchable*, and it thereby burns the damned *forever*. The tortures doled out by demons don't ever pause, and Satan never tires of masticating the vicious. Hell is a place of pain without end.

We mentioned in chapter 2 that we do not believe in hell. We also believe that a just God would not ever make such a place. Hell is immoral. We also said in chapter 4 that the motive to avoid going to hell cannot be the basis for morality because it disrupts properly moral motivation. The threat of eternal punishment skews our normal moral reasoning—if you think that eternal consequences hang for you in your decisions, you may end up doing good things, but you'll likely be doing them for the wrong reasons, namely, to save your hide. Hell, if it exists, is unjust; moreover, as we said, the very notion of hell is morally pernicious. Yet many religious believers hold that hell exists and that God actually damns souls. How can belief in eternal torment be reconciled with belief in a just God? That's the problem of hell.

Let us try to be more explicit. The problem of hell arises from a group of commonly held beliefs that, though popular, are in tension with each other. They are, roughly:

Hell is a place where the damned are punished.

The punishment of the damned is that of eternal torment.

The damned are punished in retribution for their wrongs.

All retributive punishment must be proportionate to the wrong occasioning the punishment.

Humans are incapable of inflicting infinite harm, but the damned receive infinite punishment.

One of these propositions must be rejected if hell is to be just. Think of something you've done that was wrong. Maybe you stole some bubble gum from the corner store when you were a kid. Maybe you told a fib about yourself as an adolescent to impress your friends. Maybe as an adult, you were rude and ungrateful to someone who did you a favor. If you haven't committed any of these errors in particular, simply consider some other case in which you did something wrong but of small significance. Now imagine you had been caught in the act, and the punishment for your minor infraction was *a full week of beatings.* You'd be taken to a remote location, where nobody can hear you scream, and you will be flogged, whipped, pummeled, and beaten for seven days straight. This punishment, surely, is too severe for the moral wrong we are imagining. Such a severe and prolonged punishment does not fit any of these crimes.

Anyone who thinks that corporal punishment is appropriate also thinks that such punishment must only be as severe as the wrong committed. The more severe the crime, the more times the paddle comes down. But, if punishment is to be just, those who dole out the punishment must not paddle excessively. Of course, in specific cases there may be room for judgment on the part of those who punish: does a fib deserve three, five, or ten whacks of the paddle? Is a fib from an adolescent worse than theft by a young child? And so on. But no matter how these judgments are decided, it is well outside the range of justice to say a young child deserves a week of beating for stealing a pack of bubble gum, an adolescent needs a month of whipping for a lie, or a young adult needs a full 168 hours of paddling for being rude.

To be sure, we are not denying that each of these are cases of moral wrongdoing. Nor are we denying that retributive and corporal punishment are sometimes appropriate (though we do have concerns about corporal punishment's effects on those who administer it). What we are saying is that punishment must be proportionate, otherwise it is unjust. A week of severe beatings for a minor moral infraction is therefore unjust.

For the sake of argument, we are willing to concede that there are crimes that may merit a full weeklong beating. There may even be crimes worth months-, years-, or even decades-long beatings. Again, we are not denying that there are cases in which retributive corporal punishment is morally appropriate. Yet it seems clear that there are no crimes worthy of an *eternal* beating because there are no crimes that are *infinitely harmful*. Humans can do serious and lasting harm to themselves, each other, and the environment, but none of these harms are ever extensive enough to merit *infinite* punishment. We are finite creatures, and our powers are too small to do infinite harm. Moreover, even in the cases of serious wrongs we can commit, the harm we do is limited. Take for example, mass murder. Mass murder is among the worst things a human can do. Yet even in the most horrific acts of genocide, the harm that is done is finite. The appropriate punishment for even the most extreme moral wrongdoing must itself be finite.

Not only are humans limited in terms of their capacity to harm, but the universe is filled with a finite number of things that can be harmed in a morally significant way. If there were an evil scientist who found a way to kill all living things on Earth, he or she would still be guilty of killing a finite number of things. He or she would have committed a massive, mind-bogglingly horrendous moral wrong, but nonetheless he or she would be guilty of a finite amount of harm. Accordingly, the evil scientist would deserve highly severe and long-lasting punishment, but not infinite punishment. But, again, hell is a place of infinite punishment. How could hell possibly be just?

It may be countered that the infinity of harm is not to be found here in the world, but in God. The wrong done in turning one's back on God, not following His commandments, not reciprocating His love, and not living as He had made us, perhaps, does great harm. Perhaps it is infinitely wrong to reject or defy God.

There is something going for this reply. God, if He exists, is supremely perfect. He, thereby, would be supremely valuable. So perhaps rejecting a life with God is an infinite error. Hell is just because it is a place where those who commit the infinite harm of rejecting God go to receive their due punishment, namely, infinite torment.

But now consider: Is God harmed when He is denied or defied? Does God suffer when His name is taken in vain? Is God diminished or hurt when people do not follow His commandments? Does one harm God when one denies His existence? No. If God manifests the omniproperties, then He must be invulnerable to harm. If God is perfect, there could be no way to detract from Him, no way to make Him less than He is; there is no way to harm God. So even if a person has erred in not embracing God and living according to His word, God has not been harmed by this error.

To be clear, God may be disappointed in us for our failures, and perhaps we severely disappoint God when we reject Him or fail to live according to His word. But surely it is overkill to say that we must suffer eternally simply for disappointing someone, no matter who that someone is. Again, take the relationship one may have with God as one of intimacy, perhaps analogous to friendship. Imagine two friends, Sam and Jake. They do many things together, and they have a real regard for each other. They perhaps go to a ball game on weekends. They also see movies together. But one day Jake finds other things to do; perhaps he starts going to concerts and stops going to ball games and movies. He no longer wants to do the things Sam most likes to do. Now, Jake is surely missing out on something—he's missing out on ball games and movies with Sam. And we may suppose that Sam surely is disappointed; from Sam's point of view, Jake is making the wrong choices concerning how and with whom to spend his time.

However, it would be morally outrageous for Sam to go out of his way to harm Jake because of this disappointment. Surely this does happen—people who once were friends become bitter enemies, jilted lovers become vengeful stalkers, and so on. But those who lash out at people with whom they are disappointed are childish egomaniacs. Part of being a grownup among other grownups is realizing that people will often change over the course of their lives, and so they will change their interests and what they do. That can be disappointing, especially when the people you love change their minds about you. In fact, it can be humiliating. However, to desire another's misery and destruction is to betray the love that should be the source of the disappointment. When you love someone, you want the best for that person, even if the best is not with you. And even if you are the best for that person and that person can't see it, you must still respect that person's choices. You can't force that person to love you and stay with you. That betrays the love, too.

Hence, the core of the problem of hell is not simply that hell is inconsistent with justice and morality. Hell is inconsistent with love. If there were a God who perfectly loved humans, wouldn't He want us to be happy, even if we chose not to live with Him or follow His word? The fact that God subjects those who break His commandments and do not love Him to everlasting punishment shows that He is not a loving God after all.

Hence, we put the question once again: How could a just and loving God create hell and send people there for eternity?

One might respond that God does not *send* people to hell but only *allows* people to choose hell. It may be said that hell is not a place of punishment but rather a place where people get what they want, namely, to be away from God and with their vices. This is one way to interpret Dante's *Inferno*, where those in hell have chosen to be there. In fact, in Dante, the damned choose what their torments will be. The lustful are blown about by changing winds, the violent and wrathful are put to pounding each other for eternity, and the gluttonous wallow in filth like pigs. These are the lifestyles these people chose while living, and so it is the eternal afterlife they have chosen as well.

There is, again, something going for this solution. It is an ingenious strategy. Hell, in fact, is what one has chosen, and so God is actually respecting our choices in giving the damned their respective versions of eternity. But there are problems.

The first is whether the experiences in hell are actually what the people chose in life. When a glutton chooses to eat too much cake, he has chosen a few extra pieces of cake; he has not chosen to be a pig. To be sure, what he chooses can be described as *being* a pig, but he's not choosing that description. He's choosing the cake. When someone else, a wrathful person, decides that she must respond with force to an insult, she is choosing to punch a rude person in the nose. What she is doing can be described as *being a* berserk maniac. But she's not choosing to be a berserker; she's choosing to punch a rude person.

What is required to respect a person's choices is to allow her what she chose as she chose it, not as you see it. For example, we, the authors, cannot stand it when people wear baseball hats sideways or backward. To us, it looks very silly to wear hats that way. Clearly most people who wear their hats that way don't choose that style because it looks silly, but rather because they believe it says of them that they have certain urban sensibilities. Or perhaps they believe it gives them a playful and unruly look. Were they to receive what they've chosen, it would not be a lop-sided and stupid-looking hat (which is how *we* see it), but a hat that fits with their sense of style.

Hell, so described, runs afoul of this requirement. If hell is what people choose, and if God is respecting our choices by allowing some to go there, then hell must reflect what people chose as they chose it, not how what they chose would be described by someone else. Otherwise hell is punishment again. And if hell is eternal punishment, it is unjust.

Again, the problem of hell is not an argument for atheism. Instead, it is a philosophical puzzle that those theists who believe in hell must grapple with.

THE RELIGION AND MORALITY TEST

We have argued in the main text that people can be moral without the aid of a religious tradition; the human capacity for moral reasoning works independently of our religious commitments. Religion does not provide a basis for morality. The following test, we think, can help show this. For the test to work correctly, you've got to follow a few ground rules. First, you must work through the following considerations in the assigned order. Don't read Part II until you've finished all the tasks in Part I. Second, give your honest responses to the questions in the tasks.

PART I

Imagine that we Earthlings have made first contact with an alien species, the Zanons, on a distant planet. We are able to communicate with them via interplanetary e-mail. They are technologically more advanced than us, and they have spaceships capable of reaching Earth in about five Earth years. They tell us they are coming, and knowing that we might be wary of them, they tell us that they are a deeply religious people whose morality is grounded in the divine word of Zeus. In fact, we find out that a good deal of their religion has deep resonance with Greek Olympian mythology. They send their sacred books to us as an attachment to their final e-mail, and they board their spaceships heading for Earth. Many here eagerly read the books, and they find among their stories the following strange tales and prescriptions:

(1) **Agamemnon's sacrifice:** Agamemnon was a military commander, and he asked Zeus to grant him victory over the Setinomma. "If thou wilt deliver the Setinomma into my hands, then the first creature that comes out of the door of my house to meet me when I return from them in peace shall be Zeus's; I will offer that as a whole-offering." Zeus granted the victory, and upon return home, Agamemnon's only child, his daughter, came out to welcome him home. Agamemnon could not believe it and was ready to go into hiding, but his daughter admonished him: "Father, you made a vow to Zeus; do to me what you solemnly vowed. . . ." Agamemnon allowed her to mourn for two months; then he sacrificed her.

(2) **Perseus on the role of women:** Let the woman learn in silence with all subjection. But I suffer not a woman to teach, nor to usurp authority over the man, but to be in silence. For Zeon was first formed, then Pandora. And Zeon was not deceitful, but the woman [Pandora] was in the transgression [for opening the box of plagues].

(3) **Apollo on slavery:** Slaves, obey your earthly masters with fear and trembling and with a sincere heart as you would Zeus, not by the way of eye service, as people pleasers, but as slaves of Zeus, following the commands from the heart.

(4) **Menelaus's retribution:** Menelaus went up to Corinth. Along the way, children came out of the city, and they insulted him, and they said to him: "Hey, fat boy!" "Heavy load!" "Keep walking, chunky!"

Menelaus turned back and looked at them, and he cursed them in the name of Zeus. And then there came forth three cyclopes from the rocks nearby, and the cyclopes crushed the heads of twenty of the children. Menelaus then went instead to Sparta.

(5) Agamemnon's orders: Agamemnon's army warred against the Scythians, who did not worship Zeus. Zeus had commanded Agamemnon to slay all the males. And so the army slew all the kings of the Scythians . . . and they took the Scythian women and children. They burnt their cities. . . . And Agamemnon then asked them: "Did you save all the women and children? Kill every male among the children, and kill every woman that is not a virgin. But the girls that are still virgins—keep them alive for yourselves."

Let's take a moment to think about these stories and the lessons they contain. We have imagined that they belong to the mythology of a distant alien race, coming now to Earth with technology that well surpasses ours. The aliens hold that they are moral and live by the precepts of their religious traditions. What should we expect of Zanon morality, if their moral code features these stories?

We have posed versions of this test to students, family, and friends over the years, and the following little exercise is very instructive. Take a pencil and a sheet of paper and jot down three short things about each of these stories. First, write down what you think the moral lesson of the story is. Next, judge whether it is a good moral lesson. Third and finally, record why you think it is a good or bad moral lesson. It's not hard to do this; it just takes a minute or so. We've had our students do it in class many, many times. Below are some sample answers we've collected recently.

(1) Lesson: Deals with Zeus count more than duty to family. Bad lesson (but with some good), because though it is important to keep a deal, you shouldn't have to kill your daughter for it. Zeus is wrong to hold Agamemnon to it.

(2) Lesson: Women have no authority. Bad lesson, because women are equal. And women shouldn't be punished for Pandora's errors. (One female student said: I wouldn't have opened the box, so why should I be the one being punished?)

(3) Lesson: Slaves should submit to their masters. Bad, because people do not have a right to own other people.

(4) Lesson: Unclear. Maybe don't mess with Zeus's heroes, or else! Bad, but may be good, because holy men deserve respect. However, being crushed by a cyclops is overdoing the response.

(5) Lesson: Total war and genocide against enemies. Also, it looks as if Agamemnon is endorsing sex-slavery of children. This is very bad, because genocide is the mass slaughter of people who are not combatants but civilians. And sex slavery of children is wrong because it's slavery, rape, and what's worse, done to a child.

We assume your answers were similar to those above. And so we ask: What would you expect of this race of aliens? Would you, after having read the myths from which their moral norms derive, prepare to greet them with a glad heart and hopes for a peaceful future with them? Or would you worry about the Zanon morality? Given the passages, we'd worry. If these aliens follow the moral percepts presented in their holy books, we are in for a very bad time with them.

PART II

We've seen that some religions, and particularly that of our fictional alien race of Zanons, can have utterly horrible moral lessons in their holy books. Now, imagine that the Zanons finally show up here on Earth. They don't try to enslave us, and they don't already own slaves. We quickly discover, to our delight, that the Zanons are in fact opposed to slavery. Imagine further that they don't make war on us to convert us to Zeus worship. And they hold their familial bonds most seriously, they respect the rights of women, and they abhor sexual violence against children.

What a relief! Given the contents of their holy book, we had good reason to expect the worst of the Zanons. The Zanons told us that their morality comes from their religion and the stories of gods and heroes told in their holy book. But we discovered that those gods and heroes are morally repugnant. And yet the Zanons have turned out to be a morally decent people. How did the Zanons do it? It seems almost as if they are moral *despite* their religious traditions. Again, how did they pull this off?

The answer is that the Zanons are capable of moral judgment and action in roughly the same way you are. In fact, the Zanons' situation is perhaps very much like your situation. How? Here's our confession: All those stories we presented from the Zanon holy book are actually stories from the Bible. We simply changed the proper names. Here they are from the King James Version:

(1) And Jephthah vowed a vow unto the LORD, and said, If thou shalt without fail deliver the children of Ammon into mine hands, then it shall be, that whatsoever cometh forth of the doors of my house to meet me, when I return in peace from the children of Ammon, shall surely be the LORD's, and I will offer it up for a burnt offering. So Jephthah passed over unto the children of Ammon to fight against them; and the

LORD delivered them into his hands.... And Jephthah came to Mizpeh unto his house, and, behold, his daughter came out to meet him. ... And it came to pass, when he saw her, that he rent his clothes, and said, Alas, my daughter! thou hast brought me very low.... And she said unto him, My father, if thou hast opened thy mouth unto the LORD, do to me according to that which hath proceeded out of thy mouth.... And she said unto her father, Let this thing be done for me: let me alone two months, that I may go up and down upon the mountains, and bewail my virginity.... And it came to pass at the end of two months, that she returned unto her father, who did with her according to his vow which he had vowed: and she knew no man. (Judges 11:30–39)

(2) Let the woman learn in silence with all subjection. But I suffer not a woman to teach, nor to usurp authority over the man, but to be in silence. Note for Adam was first formed, then Eve. And Adam was not deceived, but the woman being deceived was in the transgression. (1 Timothy 11–14)

(3) Servants, be obedient to them that are your masters according to the flesh, with fear and trembling, in singleness of your heart, as unto Christ; not with eyeservice, as menpleasers; but as the servants of Christ, doing the will of God from the heart. (Ephesians 6:5–6)

(4) And he went up from thence unto Bethel: and as he was going up by the way, there came forth little children out of the city, and mocked him, and said unto him, Go up, thou bald head; go up, thou bald head. And he turned back, and looked on them, and cursed them in the name of the LORD. And there came forth two she bears out of the wood, and tare forty and two children of them. And he went from thence to mount Carmel, and from thence he returned to Samaria. (2 Kings 2:23–26)

(5) And they warred against the Midianites, as the LORD commanded Moses; and they slew all the males. And they slew the kings of Midian, beside the rest of them that were slain. . . . And the children of Israel took all the women of Midian captives, and their little ones, and took the spoil of all their cattle, and all their flocks, and all their goods. And they burnt all their cities wherein they dwelt. . . . And Moses said unto them, Have ye saved all the women alive? . . . Now therefore kill every male among the little ones, and kill every woman that hath known man by lying with him. But all the women children, that have not known a man by lying with him, keep alive for yourselves. (Numbers 31:7–18)

The lesson should be clear. Your sense of morality, and even your moral convictions, does not depend on the fact that you possess and regularly consult a holy book. Your reactions to the Zanon versions demonstrate that you believe that if you were to take the lessons of the Bible literally, you would not be a moral person. That is, to be a moral person, one must be able to interpret and evaluate stories in the Bible. And this requires *independent* moral judgment and deliberation. Once again, the Bible does not provide the basis for morality. At best it offers moral lessons. But we must always exercise our own moral reflection in order to evaluate those lessons.

Accordingly, when the Zanons claimed their morality comes from their holy books, they were only half right. Their moral judgments and habits came from the regular use of their rationality in thinking through and wrestling with their holy books. Whatever moral lessons they have gotten from reading their literature are actually results of their independent moral reasoning. The same, we the authors, think is true of you. Reading a Bible can be good for you, and the Bible can be a real source of inspiration. But those moments in which a moral truth emerges from thinking through a biblical passage are productions of your own moral deliberation. So how can one be moral without religion? Our answer is: in the conscientious and responsible exercise of moral reasoning. The Religion and Morality Test shows that religious believers must engage their independent capacities for moral reasoning to properly understand the moral lessons of the Bible. And consequently, religious believers must reject the thought that morality depends on religion.

WORKS CITED AND FURTHER READING

✣

Adams, Robert. *The Virtue of Faith*. Oxford: Oxford University Press, 1987.

Anselm. *Proslogion*. Notre Dame, IN: University of Notre Dame Press, 1979.

Aquinas, Thomas. *Summa Theologica*. Notre Dame, IN: Christian Classics, 1948.

Aristotle. *The Nicomachean Ethics*. Amherst, NY: Prometheus Books, 1987.

Augustine. *The City of God*. Cambridge: Cambridge University Press, 1998.

Bacon, Francis. *Novum Organum*. Chicago: Willam Benton, 1952.

Bayne, Tim, and Yujin Nagasawa. "The Grounds of Worship." *Religious Studies* (2006): 42.

Clifford, W. K. *The Ethics of Belief*. Amherst, NY: Prometheus Books, 1999.

Comfort, Ray. *God Doesn't Believe in Atheists*. South Plainfield, NJ: Bridge Publishing, 1993.

Copan, Paul, and Paul Moser, eds. *The Rationality of Theism*. New York: Routledge, 2003.

Coulter, Ann. *Godless: The Church of Liberalism*. New York: Three Rivers Press, 2007.

Dawkins, Richard. *The God Delusion*. New York: Mariner, 2006.

Dennett, Daniel. *Breaking the Spell*. New York: Penguin Books, 2006.

———. *Darwin's Dangerous Idea*. New York: Simon and Schuster, 1995.

Dostoyevsky, F. *The Brothers Karamazov*. Trans. Constance Garnett. New York: Random House, 1957.

D'Souza, Dinesh. *What's So Great about Christianity*. Washington, DC: Regenery, 2007.

Harris, Sam. *The End of Faith*. New York: Norton, 2004.

———. *Letter to a Christian Nation*. New York: Vintage, 2006.

Henry, Carl F. H. *Twilight of a Great Civilization*. Wheaton, IL: Good News Publishers, 1988.

Hick, John. *Evil and the God of Love*. 2nd ed. San Francisco: Harper and Row, 2001.

———. *Philosophy of Religion*. Englewood Cliffs, NJ: Prentice Hall, 1963.

Hitchens, Christopher. *God Is Not Great*. New York: Twelve, 2007.

Hume, David. *Dialogues Concerning Natural Religion*. Amherst, NY: Prometheus Books, 1776 [1989].

Hunsberger, Bruce E., and Bob Altenmeyer. *Atheists: A Groundbreaking Study of America's Nonbelievers*. Amherst, NY: Prometheus Books, 2006.

Kant, Immanuel. *Fundamental Principles of the Metaphysics of Morals*. Amherst, NY: Prometheus Books, 1785 [1987].

Kenny, Anthony. *What Is Faith?* Oxford: Oxford University Press, 1992.

Le Poidevin, Robin. *Arguing for Atheism*. New York: Routledge, 1996.

Lewis, C. S. "On Obstinancy in Belief." *Sewanee Review* 63 (1955): 522–38.

Linker, Damon. "Atheism's Wrong Turn." *New Republic*, December 10, 2007.

Locke, John. *Second Treatise of Government*. Amherst, NY: Prometheus Books, 1690 [1986].

Maimonides, Moses. *The Guide for the Perplexed*. Chicago: University of Chicago Press, 1963.

Mill, John Stuart. *On Liberty*. Amherst, NY: Prometheus Books, 1859 [1986].

———. *Utilitarianism*. Amherst, NY: Prometheus Books, 1861 [1987].

Onfray, Michel. *Atheist Manifesto*. Trans. Jeremy Leggatt. New York: Arcade Publishing, 2005.

Packer, J. I. *Knowing God*. Downer's Grove, IL: InterVarsity Press, 1973.

Paley, William. *Evidences of the Existence and Attributes of the Deity*. New York: Free Press, 1802 [1965].

Plato. *Euthyphro, Apology, Crito*. Amherst, NY: Prometheus Books, 1988.

Ross, W. D. *The Right and the Good*. Indianapolis: Hackett, 1930.

Russell, Bertrand. *Why I Am Not a Christian*. New York: Simon and Schuster, 1957.

Schlessinger, Laura, and Stewart Vogel. *The Ten Commandments: The Significance of God's Laws in Everyday Life.* New York: HarperCollins, 1998.

Spinoza, Baruch. *Ethics.* Amherst, NY: Prometheus Books, 1677 [1989].

Sunstein, Cass. *Going to Extremes.* New York: Oxford University Press, 2009.

Thrower, James. *Western Atheism: A Short History.* Amherst, NY: Prometheus Books, 2000.

Wallis, Jim. *God's Politics.* San Francisco: Harper, 2005.

Wolterstorff, Nicholas. *Reason within the Bounds of Religion.* Grand Rapids, MI: Eerdmans, 1976.

Zacharias, Ravi. *A Shattered Visage: The Real Face of Atheism.* Grand Rapids, MI: Baker Books, 1990.

INDEX

abortion, 102
Abraham, 43, 46–47, 148
accommodationism, 91–93
Adam, 138, 206
Agamemnon, 202–204
agreement, 23–24, 39, 104, 116, 148
Allen, Woody, 16–17
Anselm of Canterbury, 85, 151, 209
antitheists, 92
Apollo, 202
Aquinas, St. Thomas, 117, 122, 209
argument, 10–12, 15–19, 21–27,
    32–34, 36–41, 49, 50, 54,
    56–63, 72–88, 91–95, 100,
    103–11, 127, 141–42, 147, 155,
    157, 159–64, 166–67, 176, 183,
    186, 189, 191–92, 195, 199; *ad
    hominem*, 76; counterargument,
    55; as diagnostic, 33, 39; *Presto!*
    arguments, 57–60, 62–63, 111;
    ontological, 79–86, 154
Aristotle, 122
Arkansas Constitution, 69
atheism, 9, 11, 12, 41, 67, 70–71, 86,
    90–91, 95–97, 117, 127–28,

141, 145–48, 162–66, 191, 199,
    210–11; atheist as pothole,
    46–47; definition of, 43–66
Auschwitz, 164
autonomy, 127, 164, 167

Babylonian Talmud, 160
Bacon, Francis, 121, 209
Bayne, Tim, 164, 209
belief, 9–13, 17, 19–27, 30–37,
    39–41, 43–44, 46–47, 49,
    53–57, 62–63, 69–72, 76, 79,
    85–96, 127–28, 130–31, 140,
    142, 144–49, 162–64, 166, 183,
    185, 188, 191, 194, 210; belief
    evaluation, 34–35, 38, 55, 68;
    core, 19–21, 24; ethics of,
    50–53, 55–56, 62, 65, 90, 95,
    184, 209; momentous beliefs,
    37, 39
Benedict (pope), 164
Bible, 50, 68, 97, 129, 137, 140, 175,
    178–79, 182, 205, 207–208
biblical references, 67, 98, 114, 115,
    116, 152, 164, 193, 206, 207

big questions, 64, 177
Bill of Rights, 168, 174
Blake, Daniel, 164
Buddhism, 43, 187

charity, 105–106
Christ, 115, 206
Christianity, 20, 43–44, 46, 50, 164,
    167, 209; Christians, 45–46, 69,
    90, 97, 116, 133, 167, 182, 187–
    89, 209–10
Christian Liberation Theology, 188
Clifford, W. K., 52, 144, 209
commands/commandments, 97–98,
    100, 101, 103, 105–11, 114,
    115, 117, 122, 141, 149, 151,
    153, 156–57, 160, 166, 196,
    198, 203, 207; Ten Command-
    ments, 97–98, 100, 106, 110–
    11, 156, 166, 196, 198, 211
Confucianism/Confucians, 44, 167
consolation, 145–46
Constitution, US, 68–70, 168–69,
    177–81, 190
core beliefs, 19–21, 24
Coulter, Ann, 100, 209
cosmological argument, 58, 62

Dante Alighieri, 193, 198
Dawkins, Richard, 71, 77, 82–84, 89,
    209
Declaration of Independence, 171, 177

democratic/democracy, 9, 27, 35–36,
    54, 164, 174, 178, 190–91;
    ancient democracy, 168–69;
    constitutional democracy,
    168–69, 173, 177, 179–81
denial, 47, 49, 138
Dennett, Daniel, 71, 77, 81–82, 209
Deontology, 120–22, 124, 167, 170
dignity, 163, 165, 167, 184
disagreement, 11, 15–30, 32–37,
    39–41, 45, 51, 55, 57, 72–75,
    77, 86, 104, 118, 125, 160, 167,
    184, 191; momentous, 19, 39,
    72; no sweat disagreements,
    17–19, 73
disengagement, 11
Divine Law, 122, 160
Dostoevsky, Fyodor, 97
D'Souza, Dinesh, 97–100, 102, 111,
    141, 145–46, 209

Eden, 137–38
Egyptians, 116; sun god (Ra), 190
Ephesians 6:5–6, 115, 206
Epicurean, 119
ethics, 90, 117–18, 122–24; 209,
    211; of belief, 50–53, 55–56, 62,
    65, 95, 184, 209; of citizenship,
    178, 180–83, 185–89, 209
Eudaimonism, 121–22
euthanasia, 29, 102
Euthyphro's dilemma, 104–106

evaluation, 22, 34, 50–51, 65; belief evaluation, 34–35, 38, 68, 93; moral evaluation, 134, 151, 155
Eve, 138, 206
evidence, 18–19, 21–22, 29–35, 37, 39, 49–57, 72–73, 92–95, 179, 210
evidentialism, 162
evil, 11, 45, 65, 68, 77, 88, 91–92, 95–96, 100, 105, 115, 124–25, 165–66, 170, 210; evil scientist, 196; problem of/theodicy, 127–35, 137–47, 155, 162
Exodus 22:18, 98

faith, 12, 21–22, 77, 86, 129, 140, 163, 167, 186, 209–10; blind faith, 162; faithful, 68, 71
Fallen world–ism, 137–38
free and equal treatment, 171–82, 189, 191
freedom, of conscience, 70, 117; human freedom, 134–36, 144, 164, 166–67, 169; intellectual, 94, 174; political, 117, 143, 168, 171–75, 177, 179, 188–89
free exercise of religion, 182–86
friendship, 147, 158, 197
forced intimacy, 152–53, 187
Ford, Harrison, 30–32
foundational claim, 82, 88, 96–118, 124–25, 140–42, 155, 166

gluttony, 198
God: existence of, 11, 41, 45–50, 57–64, 67–69, 79–81, 83–86, 92, 127, 130–32, 137, 141–44, 147, 149, 156, 191–92; as ground of morality, 82, 88, 96–118, 124–25, 140–42, 155, 166; as moral guide, 102–103, 107, 115–16, 141
golden rule, 111–13
government neutrality, 174, 177, 178
Graham, Billy, 129, 131, 146, 164
Greeks, 60, 115–19, 121–22, 125, 201
group polarization, 36

Han Solo, 30–32
Harris, Sam, 71, 77, 86, 89, 209
hedonism/hedonists, 119, 120, 124, 187
Hell, 49, 96–98, 144, 175, 193–99
Henry, Carl F. H., 141, 210
Hick, John, 133, 210
Hinduism, 44
Hitchens, Christopher, 71, 77, 80–81, 89, 210
Hume, David, 60, 210

individual liberty, 38, 167, 169–70
Irenaeus, 133
Isaiah 58:10–11, 164
Islam, 43

Jefferson, Thomas, 169–72
Jephthah, 205–206
Jesus, 20, 45–46, 98, 115, 136, 140,
    167, 193
Jews/Jewish, 167, 187, 189
Job, 129, 137–38; 38:2, 152; 40:7–8,
    152
Judaism, 43, 167, 176, 187, 189
Judges 11:30–39, 206
justification, 30–32, 34, 87, 93, 107,
    122, 125, 134; political justifica-
    tion, 171–74, 178–81, 185, 187

Kant, Immanuel, 121, 210
Katrina, hurricane, 129, 164
2 Kings 2:23–26, 206

Letterman, David, 108
Linker, Damon, 72, 210
Locke, John, 169–70, 172, 210
Luke 14:26, 115

Maimonides, 161–63, 210
Mark 9:42, 193; 10:1–12, 98
Marx, Karl, 188–90
Matthew 5:31, 98
Menelaus, 202–203
Mill, John Stuart—Mill's principle,
    37–38, 210
modal logic, 82–84
Mom's Maxim, 15, 20–28, 37–40, 55
Montana, 190

moral/morality, 9, 11–13, 15, 20–21,
    24–25, 29–30, 37, 41, 45, 49, 53,
    55, 65–67, 69, 71, 77, 86–93,
    95–120, 122–25, 127–31, 133–
    52, 154–55, 157, 159, 162–68,
    173, 175–77, 180–85, 187–89,
    191–98, 201, 203–205, 207–208,
    210; moral principles, 11, 97, 102,
    123, 142; moral agent, 99–102,
    115, 148, 150–51, 157, 159;
    moral autonomy, 127; moral
    commitments of atheists, 95;
    moral indifference, 142, 144;
    morality and the new atheism, 86;
    moral judgments/evaluations,
    64–65; moral quietism, 142, 144;
    moral responsibility, 9, 138–39,
    150, 167; moral standing, 20, 150
Moses, 98, 161, 207, 209, 210
murder, 30, 90, 97–98, 106–107,
    109–11, 117, 135, 177, 195
Muslims, 167, 187, 189
Mysterianism, 62–63, 138–40
mystery, 62–64, 129, 138–40, 145

Nagasawa, Yujin, 164, 209
New Atheists, 11, 66–67, 69, 71–94
New Testament, 97
9/11 attacks, 128–29, 131
No Reasonable Opposition strategy,
    27–29, 32, 34–37, 47, 55–57,
    68, 71, 78, 86

no sweat disagreements, 17–19, 73

Numbers 31:7–18, 207

obedience, 114, 117, 151; complete obedience, 160

objectivity, 11, 17, 65, 75, 88, 90, 95–96, 101, 103, 108–10, 113, 118, 123–25, 127, 145, 165–66

obligation, 53, 78, 86, 89, 103, 124, 153, 160, 165, 182, 185–88; to worship, 148–50, 154, 156, 159, 162

Old Testament, 67, 97

Olympian, 116, 201

Onfray, Michael, 71, 77, 89–90, 210

Packer, J. I., 101, 210

Paley, William, 60, 210

Parable of Tom, 73–75

Paul, Apostle, 97–98, 115–17, 125

permissibility, 29, 75, 77–78, 175, 177–78, 183, 185, 188

Perseus, 202

piety/pious, 104–105

Plato, 32, 104, 166, 210

pluralism, 123–24

politeness, 15, 21–22, 38–39, 74–75, 120

politics, 9, 12, 15, 20–21, 24–30, 37, 40, 76, 162, 164, 189, 191, 211

pope, 177, 180–81

Presto! arguments, 57–60, 62–63, 111

problem of evil/theodicy, 127–35,

137–47, 155, 162; problem of privacy, 155, 164; problem of worship, 13, 147–63

proportionate punishment, 194–95

Proslogion, 151, 209

prudent, 99

Psalms 53:1–5, 67; Psalmist, 67–68

Ra, Egyptian Sun God, 190

Rakitin, 97

rational agents, 33, 94

reasons, 11–12, 16, 20–24, 31–41, 49–54, 63–64, 68, 72–75, 79, 83, 88, 92, 97–99, 109–11, 117, 128, 137–38, 141, 147, 149–51, 154–59, 162, 171–73, 178–88, 193, 207–208; reasonable, 33–39, 41, 51, 56–57, 72–73, 75, 86–87, 91, 93–95, 104, 118, 128, 164–65, 167–68, 191–92; see also *no reasonable opposition*

relativism, 18, 22, 29–30, 88, 95–96, 112–13, 141, 177

religion, 9–10, 12–13, 15, 20–21, 24–30, 37, 40, 44–47, 60, 71, 86–87, 89, 91, 115, 143–44, 148, 188, 201, 205, 208, 210–11; as basis of morality, 166; free exercise of, 182, 186; in politics, 165–68, 176–77, 189, 191

religious, worldview, 88; exemptions, 185

respect, treat others with, 10–12, 25, 38–41, 55, 72, 74–77, 91, 120, 122–23, 128, 136, 141, 144, 155, 164, 167–68, 172, 174–75, 177, 183, 188, 191, 197–99, 204–205

retributive punishment, 194–95

Revelationism, 138–40

Romans, 119, 125; 2:14–15, 116–17

Rome, 119, 121

Ross, W. D., 123, 210

Russell, Bertrand, 127, 210

Samuel, 114–15; I Samuel 15:3–22, 114

satan, 149, 187, 193; satanic, 188; Satanist, 189–90

Saturn, 108

Saul, 114–15

Schlessinger, Laura, 100, 103, 211

Scorsese, Martin, 16

secularism, 70, 90, 183; secular, 120, 124–25, 178; secular politics, 191

semantic saturation, 23

Shmod, 58, 61

slavery, 100, 115, 119, 152–53, 168, 202, 204–205

Socrates, 74, 104, 106, 108–10

stem cells, 29, 180–84

subjectivity, 101, 103, 108–10, 124

Sunstein, Cass, 36, 211

Talmud, 160

Taoism, 44; Taoists, 167

teleological argument, 60, 62

Ten Commandments, 97–98, 100, 106, 110–11, 156, 166, 196, 198, 211

Tennessee State Constitution, 68

theism, 43–44, 145, 147–48, 154, 163, 209

theodicy/problem of evil, 127–35, 137–47, 155, 162; as biblical solution, 137–40, 144; as free-will defense, 134–37, 144; as making of good, 133; as privation of being, 132; as rationalizing evil, 142

Thor, 46

I Timothy 2:11–14, 98; 11:14, 206

tone, 68, 71–72, 74–78

Torah, 161

truth, 11, 15, 17, 19–23, 25, 28, 30–39, 50–51, 56, 60, 77, 79, 102–103, 108–10, 113, 117, 120, 122–24, 137, 155, 165, 207

tsunami of 2004, 128, 131, 134–35, 137–38, 144, 146

United States, 9–10, 27, 70, 168–69, 183, 189–90

unspoken/suppressed premise, 58–61

Utilitarianism, 119, 210

INDEX

virtue ethics, 122, 124, 157
Vogel, Stewart, 100, 211

Wallis, Jim, 143–44, 211
W-properties, 154–56, 161–62
wrath, 50, 198

Zacharias, Ravi, 141, 211
Zanons, 201, 205, 207
Zeus, 201–205

CPSIA information can be obtained
at www.ICGtesting.com
Printed in the USA
BVHW082306200721
612086BV00002B/114